a treasure trove of gems

dedication

i dedicate this book to three special and very precious gems, my granddaughters, natalie, kelsey and courtney. i feel so blessed to have you in my life. may your inner lights always shine and may joy and laughter fill your lives.

also by barbara mcdougall

tara, emissary of light
a crack in the cosmic window
gaia, our precious planet
a great cosmic joke

A Treasure Trove of Gems

Barbara McDougall

The Oracle Press

The Oracle Press
P.O. Box 121 Montville Qld 4560 Australia

National Library of Australia

ISBN 1 876494 23 9

Printed by Watson Ferguson & Co., Moorooka, Qld. 4105

acknowledgements

I wish to firstly acknowledge all my readers who have given me so much encouragement to keep on with my storytelling. I love receiving your letters and rejoice when you say that my books have brought joy and understanding into your lives. Thank you so much for your kind words. They truly warm my heart.

Secondly, I would like to acknowledge my husband, Bruce, who has been urging me for two years to put these stories into book form. I didn't take his advice at first, having my own rather stubborn agenda. However, I now feel it's time to act on his suggestion. Each time I would receive a story through me he would ask me to read it to him and he felt its impact, not only within his heart but also because they touched his soul. The stories are still coming through, so there is likely to be a storybook number two at some time in the future. I won't procrastinate so long with the next one!

I would like to acknowledge my mother, a very, very special lady, who has also been encouraging me to put the short stories into book form. She is one of my greatest admirers and proudly distributes my books to her senior citizen friends. Thanks so much Mum for your loving support.

A big 'thank you' to all my students who give me great feedback when I read the stories to them in class. Some are deeply moved, some even to tears, with the impact of them – usually tears of joy. They have suggested that I put some of the stories on CD and I have made the first steps towards this project.

I also want to thank Brian Priest, Editor of *The Oracle Press*, who so willingly and capably puts my books together for me. It is because of his help that the books take form.

Finally, I wish to acknowledge the higher aspects of myself that impulse me to write. It is such a pleasure and a joy for me and because I feel that joy within me I know that my readers will also connect with that as well. I do hope that you, the reader, will feel nourished by these stories and that they may enrich your life in many ways.

Introduction

Some years ago, during my regular morning mediation practice, I began receiving messages from higher aspects of myself, asking me to write down that which I was hearing in my head. This I did, using my non-dominant hand – my left hand. I had trained myself to hand write this way over the previous few years in an effort to slow down my turbulent and scattered mind. The process worked, along with the practice of meditation. I had suffered from mental stress and breakdowns at different times in my life and was not willing to go along that path again. Therefore, I took personal responsibility for re-training my mind.

Meditation and the left handed writing were two practical disciplines that really worked for me. Both required focus and I wasn't very good at that, however, through much practice I have also been able to achieve that state.

My books are the result of that re-training. The gift of writing in a simple yet profound way is something that lay dormant for most of my life and has now broken out from its hiding place! I feel truly blessed to be able to pass on this gift to those who choose to read. It is my hope that the work inspires you to open hidden doorways in your psyche so that your own personal gifts and talents can be shared with others.

My inner guidance is propelling me ever onward and the current challenge is to do the cover for this book myself! Considering I can only draw stick figures this is really quite a Cosmic Joke. However, I figure that if my granddaughter Natalie could produce the painting at three and a half, which became the cover of my book, *Gaia*, then surely I can do the same!

Each story in this book contains a very pertinent message. They can be read and enjoyed by anyone from around 12 years of age onward. Most of the stories are parables with many deeper meanings for those who want to delve. The words and the meanings will be felt as an internal experience. It is with the greatest of pleasure that I offer them to you and it is my great hope that they will touch you on many levels and open up doors of perception to other realities.

contents

amanda

It was a beautiful spring morning when Amanda awakened. The birds were singing sweetly and the sun was shining warmly. Amanda felt so good that she jumped out of bed and went outside in the garden. She smelt the fragrance of the flowers and felt the soft, green grass underneath her feet.

She noticed a blackbird sitting on a branch quite close to her. It was making sounds that seemed to be calling her. She listened attentively and the bird seemed to be calling her name. AM... AN... DA.

The bird then turned around and flew to another branch a little further away, then looked back to see if Amanda was following. The bird then flew on to another branch, then another, as Amanda followed, quite intrigued by this.

The bird increased the pace and Amanda found herself almost running in pursuit of the bird. She found herself out in a field where there were no houses but she wasn't afraid because she realised the blackbird was taking her somewhere that she needed to go.

The bird then flew into a clump of trees with Amanda following close behind. There in front of her eyes Amanda saw the most amazing sight. A group of blackbirds, perhaps 10 or more, were clustered together around a young child. They were protecting the child from insects and small animals that might crawl over her body. The small child appeared asleep but when Amanda tried to awaken her she didn't stir. She was breathing and looked quite peaceful, but very, very pale.

Amanda realised the young girl was hurt somehow and needed attention so she quietly asked the birds to stay with the child and keep on protecting her whilst she ran to get help.

Amanda ran all the way home and wakened her sleeping parents and told them what she had discovered in the woods. Amanda's parents rang a doctor, then prepared a stretcher with some blankets and hastily went to help the young injured girl.

All the birds flew away to a high branch as Amanda and her parents reached the injured child but Amanda quietly thanked them all for their efforts in keeping guard over the child and coming to her to get help.

The young girl recovered very quickly after spending a few days in bed. Amanda learned to trust the birds – to watch them closely with a far deeper understanding and appreciation of them to what she had known before. She realised they have an intelligence just as we have an intelligence and that they are on this Earth for a purpose just as we are.

Amanda's understanding of the Universe, and each species' role, increased rapidly after her amazing adventure with the blackbird. She felt so grateful for the experience.

Harold and James

There was once a small child and his name was Harold. Harold loved playing with the gnomes, elves and nature spirits in the bottom of the garden. He didn't have any brothers and sisters but he felt happy and contented whilst playing with his playmates from another dimension. He didn't realise they were from another dimension as they were very real to him. He often wondered why his mother and father were not able to see his little playmates as he could. It seemed strange to him, however, he didn't let it bother him.

He must have been about six years old when his parents decided it was time for him to go to school. It was there that he first began playing with other boys and girls his own age.

They laughed at him when he told them about his playmates in his garden. They didn't believe him. He felt very hurt by this and then he started wondering about them himself. As he began to doubt himself he found that his old friends were not always there when he wanted them.

He still felt their presence but wasn't able to see them. His doubt had closed down a special place inside of him that allowed him to see these little nature spirits from another realm. He missed them and wondered why they had deserted him. He didn't realise it was himself and his doubts that caused them to apparently go away.

Harold grew up. He became successful in his life. He married and then had children of his own.

One of his children, a boy called James, used to play by himself at the bottom of the garden. One day he came to his Dad and told him about his playmates – those that played with him when he was in the garden.

Harold then had memories of his own childhood, how he too had loved to play with the nature spirits, how he had never felt alone and how he loved the games they all played together.

He asked his son James if he could go down to the garden to meet the nature spirits so that he too could play the games.

Harold and his son James went off together down to the bottom of the garden in order to play with the special little creatures. Harold told James what had happened to him when he went to school and how he had allowed the derision of his school friends to create doubts in his mind. He asked James to be especially aware of this when he started school and not to listen to the other children.

He asked James to always believe in what was true for him no matter what anybody else said. James agreed, and so it was.

alan's visitor

It was a cold and frosty morning when Alan awoke to find a strange apparition standing at the foot of his bed. Alan felt quite calm and not at all alarmed by this vision. He did, however, pinch himself to feel whether he really was awake.

Alan was unafraid yet very, very curious. He looked closely at the apparition noting that it was very tall, not quite solid and slightly blue in colour. It appeared to be androgynous – neither male nor female but a balanced combination of both. Alan was intrigued. The figure was quite still and allowed Alan to peruse its countenance.

Alan then formulated words in his head and mentally asked the figure the reason for its visit. Alan waited, knowing that an answer would come.

"I have come in order for you to accept and acknowledge the truth of the spirit world. I have come so that you can experience another dimension of time and space. Your third dimension is not the only realm of experience. There are many, many more. At this period in your life it is time for you to begin your journey into other dimensional realities. I come with great love and compassion and offer my support and guidance to you throughout your journey to the light of conscious understanding. Should you ever need my guidance or protection you need only to ask and I will always assist. I am from a higher dimension and able to make myself visible to you at this time because your frequency was raised during a blissful dreaming state. I will leave you now and will leave a memento of my visit so that you know for sure you are not dreaming of my presence."

Alan's heart was beating so fast and he felt very hot, yet peaceful. He felt as if something really profound had taken place, something that would lead him into totally new areas of his life. He felt joy and excitement well up inside of him. It was almost as if an opening had occurred within his heart and central core of self and new life had entered.

The apparition vanished and in its place Alan smelt a gentle fragrance. He jumped out of bed to find the source of the fragrance and found a perfect pink rose on the floor at the foot of his bed. He gently picked up the special gift and placed it over his heart. He felt his heart leap in recognition. Waves of emotion engulfed him and he found himself crying tears of gratitude and joy.

Alan's life totally changed from that moment on. He wrote about his experience in a special diary, noting the date and time. He made the decision to press the rose into his diary as a permanent reminder to him of the life-changing situation. He also decided to have a new birth chart constructed by an astrologer depicting the exact time, date and place of the momentous event. He wanted to use the chart as a guide to the new identity he felt himself to be as a result of his spiritual experience.

Alan eventually became a gentle, loving teacher of spiritual principles and practices, aiding others to open up to their multi-dimensionality. His life path opened up for him on that wonderful morning.

A Story for the New Age

Once upon a time, many, many aeons ago, beings came to this planet Earth from a far distant star system. These beings carried within them much knowledge, especially knowledge about the celestial movements of planets and star systems.

These beings were on a mission – a mission to open the hearts and minds of humans on planet Earth to higher knowledge. They knew that humans on Earth were now ready for the next stage of their evolutionary journey and they had volunteered to be the ones to bring the information into the third dimension.

As they moved into the denser frequency on planet Earth they found they needed to make many adjustments to their own energetic bodies. They felt the density of the Earth plane making them feel heavier and more and more uncomfortable. However, they were prepared for this experience so they consciously, with will and effort, adapted their frequency levels to suit those of Earth.

The information these beings carried was universal. It was a system of knowledge that all beings in different star systems use in their daily lives to access and understand their own energy. They knew and understood how the energy from the planets and star systems impinged upon them in differing ways depending on the energetic make up of the individual. This cosmic energy formed many geometric patterns, often referred to as sacred geometry, and these energy patterns from the heavens would activate the already existing energy pattern within the circuitry system of all beings. The patterns of energy contained codes and these codes could be accessed through the study of Astrology – the Universal system for understanding planetary energies.

These light beings from another dimension of time and space were excited about their mission. It was the first time they had embarked on such an expansive journey so far away from their own home. They felt privileged to be the vehicles for imparting the knowledge to such a far distant and beautiful planet.

They had been instructed to write down, in symbolic form, the knowledge that they carried so that it would be found and deciphered by humans over different periods of Earth time. They had been instructed to write their knowledge inside caves and on stone tablets so that the information would survive through many ages. They were also asked to spend time with a particular tribe in North Africa who had an intelligence level that could integrate the higher knowledge. Their mission was to instruct this tribe with some of the knowledge so that the tribal elders could then pass it on through the ages so all future generations would understand and remember.

And so the science of Astrology came to planet Earth. Over Earth time many such visits were made and much knowledge was transmitted to many indigenous people. Knowledge was also received by humans whilst in meditative and altered states. Humans were encouraged, through thought transmissions, to study the effects of the moon and her phases on the waters of Earth and on their own individual emotional natures. They were encouraged to observe the planetary movements in the heavens and become aware of how the different connections between planets travelling through the zodiac would impact them as individuals and as a collective. They were encouraged to write down, or verbally pass on, this knowledge.

And so the celestial codes have been accessed, the information is gathering momentum as more and more humans are opening up their minds to receive this higher knowledge.

This knowledge is a healing tool, one that can awaken human channels of understanding, long dormant, enabling the information to be accessed and utilised.

This healing tool is now available to all who are drawn to remember. Our genetic coding carries ancient memories of times gone by when this wonderful science was used by all. The time is fast approaching when it will be once again understood by the masses upon planet Earth and the codes unveiled and utilised for the greater benefit of humankind.

And so it was and so it is.

Betty and Mary

Once upon a time, a very long time ago, there were two sisters – quite different in personality. One sister was playful, beautiful, felt wanted and loved by her parents. The other sister, older, had not been planned. Her entry into the womb of life was a shock to her parents.

This older sister knew on a very deep level of her being that she had not been wanted. She knew that her birth would create much friction and disharmony in the lives of her parents and their families. She entered the womb with this knowledge. She had many life lessons to learn about feeling unwanted and needy of love.

The young sister, we shall call her Mary, knew she was wanted – knew she would be loved and played with, knew she would always be provided with all of life's goodies and so she was always confident about her life.

Even in the womb of her mother she had the feeling of being wanted. Her life's lessons were of a different nature to those of her older sister.

The older sister, we shall call her Betty, lost all conscious memory of why she had come into this life and what her lessons in the schoolroom of life were to involve.

Betty loved playing outside, in nature. She loved the stones from Mother Earth. She loved being on the grass and being with the flowers and the trees. She loved listening to the birds and the wind. She loved to feel the warm sun kissing her cheeks. She was a child of nature.

Mary, on the other hand, loved to play inside with all the pretty cushions and coloured materials of her Mummy's dresses. She liked to dress up in her Mummy's clothes. She liked her beauty man-made.

The two sisters had many differences. Betty always felt resentful towards her younger sister. She didn't know why. It was simply a feeling that couldn't be expressed in words. However, she dearly wanted to love her little sister and wanted to hold her and stroke her.

One day, when they had gone to the country for a holiday, Betty was told to go outside and play. She had wanted to cuddle her little one-year-old sister but was told to get out of the way instead.

She felt banished, unwanted, useless, unloved and went out into nature for solace. A big black cloud descended over Betty. A great heaviness seemed to develop all around her. She then sensed another's presence.

A man in black grabbed her from behind and put a hand over her mouth so that she couldn't cry out. He had big black boots on and a black singlet. He was playing with some part of his body which seemed to get bigger and bigger. Betty felt terrified and she wanted to cry out but couldn't because the man was so big and strong. He held her down.

She then felt such hurt and pain – her little body was racked with deep pain hurting her insides. She blacked out with the shock of this devastating trauma.

Her body had been disfigured. Her pelvis out of shape. She had blood and all this sticky, smelly stuff all over her legs. She was left in a heap like a rag doll – unwanted, unloved, and damaged physically, emotionally and mentally. The whole essence of her being was hurting. She was in such a mess.

Her Mummy came outside, screaming and shouting things like, "What have you done – what did you do this for? Oh, why has this happened to me? What will the neighbours say? What am I going to do with you? I can't tell anyone about this."

Betty, in her weakened state, began to feel that she had created this dreadful thing to happen to her. She felt responsible for causing her Mummy such anguish and pain. She felt she must be a very bad person to bring on this sadness to her Mummy. She resolved to try and be such a good girl from then on. She didn't want to upset her Mummy anymore.

Baby Mary began crying inside the house and Mummy ran off and left Betty in order to attend to Mary. Again, Betty felt abandoned, unwanted, unloved but now she also felt ashamed and guilty because somehow she had caused this dreadful thing to happen.

Another man came to look at her a little later. He carried a black bag and he really was a nice man but Betty now was so frightened of men with black that she screamed and screamed with fear. Her little body became so rigid and stiff and her bones locked into all the wrong places. Her bones near her lower back were weakened. Her left leg shrunk up so that it was shorter than the other leg. She wasn't able to talk very much because her throat seemed blocked somehow.

The young man, who was a doctor, was so sickened by what he saw that he really was sick. His stomach couldn't handle his emotions and so he brought up his last meal.

Betty's Mummy said that no one was to tell another person about this unfortunate incident. That we were all to pretend that nothing had happened. Betty had plaster put on her leg by the doctor so her Mummy had to say that she had hurt her leg.

As time went by Betty carried all the feelings inside of her that she had experienced when in her mother's womb and when the terrible incident had happened to her. She couldn't remember the incident anymore because she had blocked it from her memory. She so wanted to be good in order to please her Mother that she developed an addiction to pleasing.

She found that if she could make others happy by doing what she felt they wanted then her life would work out well. She blocked all sense of feeling from her body and her emotional nature. She became like a robot.

She grew up and decided to get married when she was quite young. She chose her husband carefully because she wanted a kind and loving man, not a dark kind of man.

However, when Betty's children had all grown up and left home, Betty started feeling very, very depressed. She started having dreadful nightmares and her face started developing red, angry rashes. She wasn't able to sleep very well. She started to feel again all the feelings she had experienced when very young. She didn't know these feelings, of course, because she had blocked them from her conscious memory.

She started feeling resentful towards her sister Mary, but didn't know why. She started feeling very needy of her husband and believed he would abandon her. She didn't know why. She started feeling great fear when around other men.

She felt weakened, sad, lonely, and felt like crying all the time. She did cry – oceans of tears, but didn't know why. Her whole life seemed hopeless, empty. She felt unloved, and very fearful. Her strength eroded. She found herself unable to do normal tasks. She had to rest every day and go to bed very early. Her whole being was going through some major experiences. She felt as if her mind was in a fog. A great mist descended upon her.

However, in the deepest recesses of her mind she knew she would come out of this dreadful place and she knew she had the means inside of herself to do this. She knew she needed to access her memory banks to find out just what was lurking there that needed to come to the surface and be faced.

She was determined to heal herself of all the darkness inside of her. She knew that if she followed modern medicine and was prescribed drugs this would only bandaid the cause of her blackness. She wanted to eradicate the weed that was the cause of her problems.

She started learning astrology and metaphysical sciences. It was very difficult for her to study as her mind was in such a fog, but she persisted. She was determined to recover her health, her vitality and her enthusiasm for living.

She also went to alternate healers – those people who were being drawn to healing through natural means.

All these processes helped her to activate and bring to conscious awareness the deep pain and hurt she experienced in the womb and in her early childhood. She was then able to face her issues and see where the black feelings had come from. She was able to express all her dark feelings responsibly, not dumping them on others and not blaming others for them, just being able to accept that she had created them in order to learn about herself in order to clear some karmic debts.

She was able to see clearly why she felt resentful to Mary and to clear those dark feelings from her emotional body. She was able to give up her addiction to pleasing others and is now able to please herself. This way she is happy because she is now doing what she loves to do with her life rather than doing what she thinks she 'should' do.

So Betty and Mary lived happily ever after.

Fairies

Once upon a time, in the magical land of Nod, lived two little fairies. Their names were Petal and Bluebell. They loved dancing and singing on the tops of the flowers and they loved to smell the perfume of the flowers. They were happy, free spirits until one day the wicked witch from the north came into their field.

This wicked witch, Ardartha, was mean, greedy, ugly and nasty. She wanted to own the fairies' field. She wanted all the plants and trees for herself. She didn't want anyone else to share her space.

She screamed and yelled at the fairies, sending great clouds of darkness over them. They were trembling and afraid. They had never encountered such an evil thing before. They didn't understand why this bad thing was happening to them.

Petal and Bluebell had played in this field all their lives – it was their home and they knew no other. They were frightened to venture out into the big wide world and leave the safety and security of their home.

The wicked witch, Ardartha, had made her plans and they did not include Petal and Bluebell. She schemed and plotted and became nastier and nastier.

She wanted them out of her property – out of her sight.

Petal and Bluebell became more and more afraid. It was now scary for them to stay where they were and just as scary to go on to a strange place.

The wicked witch, Ardartha, began controlling the fairies, telling them what they could and couldn't do. She restricted their movements. They did not feel like free spirits any more.

Petal and Bluebell talked the situation over and realised they were becoming more and more frightened the longer they stayed in their field. Their once happy and joyful life was now a misery. They decided it was time to move out – to take a big step forward in their life and go to another field. They knew it wouldn't be the same as their home, but it seemed they had no alternative but to move on.

They lovingly whispered their goodbyes to all their friends, the plants, insects and trees, and with tears in their eyes, left the field to venture out beyond their old forms of security.

It was so scary at first, however, the sun was shining and the birds were singing. A little willy wagtail kept on chirping and singing beside them and they realised he might be attempting to show them something, so they began to follow him, feeling suddenly quite adventurous and even excited. They were on a new path and they were following their guide. They had to keep their eyes on the bird so that they didn't go off track and this required discipline and will. However, the time came when the bird came to rest on a large rock.

The two fairies looked around. There were so many flowers, insects and birds here. It was a beautiful place. All the creatures and flowers welcomed them warmly, inviting them to share their home.

How wonderful Petal and Bluebell felt. They felt warm inside their hearts – all the coldness and fear had gone. They had found their new home. Because they had moved into their fear of the unknown they had come out the other side into happiness and light.

Should similar circumstances ever happen again in their lives they would not procrastinate, just simply face their fears and move through them, as they knew they would find wonderful results on the other side.

Jeanette

Once upon a time a beautiful woman called Jeanette was sitting at her desk, gazing out towards the mountains, yearningly. She had visions of herself walking the high slopes with her dog, Tui, singing songs of praise and gratitude for all the abundance she had in her life.

Jeanette felt imprisoned in her home office. She had much work to do and she loved her work but somehow she seemed to over commit herself and didn't allow herself free playtime.

After some years of this total focus on her work she began to feel resentful towards her clients. They supported her by providing more and more work for her, for which she was grateful, but she hadn't learned to achieve balance in her life. The resentment she was feeling grew stronger and stronger and she began to send out this energy to her clients. They could feel it by the tone of her voice and the words she was using.

She was fortunate because one of her clients was a close friend who could see what was happening and she decided to talk to Jeanette. Jeanette, of course, didn't want to listen at first. She had become so hyped up from her continual focus on work to the detriment of her private life that she wasn't able to calm her nervous energy sufficiently to be attentive to her friend.

However, her friend persisted, quite vehemently, to the point where Jeanette reacted very emotionally and broke down, sobbing. All her pent up frustration and resentments began to be released.

After she calmed down sufficiently her friend then spoke to her lovingly and compassionately. She told Jeanette how concerned she was about her welfare and her health and how she felt Jeanette needed to take a good, long look at herself and be willing to change her lifestyle considerably.

Jeanette listened. She realised her friend was speaking wise words to her that came from her heart without any hidden agenda. She simply cared too much to see Jeanette lose the strong base she had built up for herself.

Jeanette decided to take hold of herself. She decided her life had become unfulfilling because of her total focus on her work. She decided to plan her first holiday for three years. She would take one whole month off work. She felt she wanted to go somewhere peaceful, in nature without many people around. She wanted to take Tui with her so she chose to go to the nearby mountains. She and Tui could explore them freely, with a sense of abandonment.

Her clients were all happy with her decision, as they knew she would come back with fresh, new, inspiring ideas and they were willing to wait for this.

She and Tui had a wonderful time. She discovered that she loved to compose songs. They would simply come into her head as she was walking through the trees. She sang her songs joyfully as she and Tui tramped through the hills. She felt a great peace and calm descend upon her whenever she was composing and singing her songs. This felt so good to her that she committed to continue this practice when she returned home. The vision she had experienced such a long time ago had come to fruition.

When her holiday ended Jeanette returned home to her work. She rearranged her daily schedule so that she and Tui could go for a walk in the hills most mornings. She arose one hour earlier in order to do this and both she and her dog benefited through the exercise and contact with nature.

Her clients also benefited as well as she always seemed to come up with really bright ideas to help them when she was walking. Because she chose to bring more balance and beauty into her life she felt happier and more fulfilled. She was always aware of when the dark feelings began to rise up inside of her and dealt with them appropriately. She knew it was break time from work when this happened.

Her life and her business thrived and her songs began to be requested by many people.

She was well content.

the twins

Once upon a time, a very long time ago, Jim and Paula used to play with the nature spirits in the bottom of their garden. Jim and Paula lived in a country that was green and lush most of the year. There was abundant rainfall and many hot days. Their garden grew prolifically. There were lots of vegetables, flowering trees and fruit trees. The garden was abundant with the fruits of nature.

Jim and Paula often watched the nature spirits going about their work. They always seemed to be busy, helping the plants to grow and receive nourishment. The little creatures often played with Jim and Paula when they had a break from their work and all parties enjoyed the fun and games they played together.

Jim and Paula's childhood was idyllic. Their parents, both writers, allowed the children a great deal of freedom, yet also set firm guidelines and parameters for them. The children felt secure with this upbringing and respected their parents' boundaries.

In a small village, quite close to where Jim and Paula lived, was another pair of twins. These children had a totally different upbringing to that of Jim and

Paula. Their parents lived a very cold and unloving life. They went out to work each day taking their twins to carers – people who earned their money by taking care of other people's children.

John and Judith did not experience the freedom of creative expression nor did they experience the pleasure of playing outside in nature. They spent their childhood cooped up inside four walls. They lived a very regimented and controlled life. Their parents loved them but their focus was on material endeavors. They worked hard but didn't know how to play. They shut down that joy place inside their heart and put up shutters and barriers instead. This is why they were cold and aloof. They allowed all joy and pleasure of living to drain from them.

Both sets of twins grew up and attended the local school. As they were the same age they were placed in the same grade. It was unusual to have two sets of twins in the same grade in such a small school so they very quickly got to know each other.

John and Judith were by this time very inhibited in their thoughts, feelings and actions. They acted stiffly and cautiously in all that they did. They felt great fear about playing outside at break times, thinking all sorts of scary things might happen to them.

Jim and Paula were open, loving and spontaneous children. They didn't like to see John and Judith so restricted and limited in their thoughts and actions, so they asked if they would like to come and visit after school.

Jim and Paula spoke such warm words of welcome and spoke excitedly about their wonderful garden that

John and Judith's curiosity was aroused. They spoke to their parents, who very willingly agreed to the plan, as they didn't want to have to look after their children when school finished.

Jim and Paula gradually awakened John and Judith to a more expansive way of being. They taught them how to love and appreciate nature and all the wondrous produce that nature provides. They taught them how to play make-believe games and then, after many months, they introduced them to their friends, the nature spirits.

At first John and Judith could only see faint outlines of the little creatures as their conditioned mind doubted their existence. However, as they opened up their mind to allow a greater degree of expansiveness their psychic abilities increased and they could then see the little creatures from another dimension.

John and Judith enjoyed their playtime after school and they began to be less and less inhibited. They were then able to show their parents, by example, how to loosen up and to relax and play more. As their parents became more relaxed life became more pleasurable for the family. They found they could all have fun together as a family and a greater degree of love and warmth permeated their hearts.

Jim and Paula lived a wonderfully happy and productive life being an inspiration and a guiding light to many people. They too became writers and were able to write about their early childhood experiences in such a way that many people were transformed through the stories. Their expansive and abundant view of life attracted expansion and abundance to them.

In the Beginning

Once upon a time, a very long time ago, there was darkness in the Universes. Only the mind of God was there. Suddenly an idea came to our Creator, a magnificent, thrilling idea.

The idea was to create light, to create energy – to create beings from that energy and so it was.

Firstly, light was created. Light is full of atomic particles, full of energy. Some of these particles merged together to form clusters. Some of the clusters grew larger and larger, forming a conglomerate mass of energy. This energy had a consciousness as it was created in the likeness of God.

These energy conglomerates grew as more particles were attracted to them. They lit up the dark sky with their brightness. Stars and planets were formed, myriads of them. Solar systems were formed with planets revolving around a central sun.

Then our Divine Creator sent out more sparks of energy so that what we call nature was formed on some of the planets and stars. Hills and valleys formed, lakes formed, and then creatures and beings developed, all in the likeness of God, that is, with all the same energy – all with a spark of the Divine within them.

Planet Earth was the most beautiful place in our solar system. It was a playground of beauty, a Garden of Eden. Many beings from other planets and star systems visited Earth. They brought much knowledge, new information and technology to the inhabitants of Earth.

Many wonderful buildings were constructed in order to keep in contact with these space visitors. The inhabitants of Earth became a highly developed civilisation, working with Universal laws direct from the Divine Creative source.

However, as time went by some of the Earthly beings became dissatisfied, possibly prompted by 'darker' beings from other places. The dissatisfaction grew and turned into frustration, which turned into anger. Many people became non-trusting, became secretive, envious and even developed hatred. The paradise that was on Earth degenerated because of the negative thoughts and feelings of some of the people.

Because the destructive energy was emitted from the people, it impregnated onto the Earth and our planet took it into herself. As the negativity developed the Earth lost some of its beauty. Some lands became eroded, rivers dried up and the soil became less fertile.

Some of the people on Earth, who were still living according to Universal, or God's law, understood what was going on. They knew that a fall from Grace was taking place and they knew that it would accelerate and grow as the people became more and more greedy, more self-centred and less interested in living in the light of understanding and love. They prayed to the Divine Creator and asked for assistance.

Then, many aeons ago, 'gods' descended to Earth. These gods were representatives of the greater Creative Being. They brought messages and instructions on how to live a peaceful and productive life.

These gods came from other planets and star systems and their information came direct from God. They had been practicing the spiritual teachings on their planets and star systems for many, many aeons. They knew that their teachings worked.

Human beings on Earth were not as evolved as these gods and were not so quick to understand the concepts. A plan was devised by the gods to interbreed with humans so that some of the spiritual teachings would become imprinted on the psyches of the humans.

This mixed race was called the 'sons of God'. They were born with higher intuitive faculties and were more in tune with the universal laws.

The sons of God developed and intermixed with human beings on Earth.

It became apparent, over time, that this intermixing was not helping human beings to evolve to a higher level of spiritual understanding about themselves so the gods from other planets and star systems who had by this time left planet Earth, decided that even more action needed to be taken.

They were concerned that the mass of humans who were so involved purely with their physical and material existence would reach a point whereby they would blow themselves and the planet up through ignorance.

A plan was developed with the full co-operation of the great Divine Principle to provide a tool, which would be instrumental in bringing human beings to a greater spiritual understanding of themselves and their place in the Universe.

The 'gods of Light' began to work on implanting a system of knowledge into man's consciousness. This system was based on the movements of the planets in a solar system. The system is called astrology. This system is used in many other parts of the galaxies and is universal in its application.

The gods of Light wrote symbols on tablets, they left writings on scrolls and carved messages into rocks. They showed how the planets and star systems are energetic bodies, each with a consciousness. The star systems have a group consciousness. All are energy.

The gods of Lights showed how these energies from the heavens impact onto humans in differing ways. They showed how humans have an opportunity to be drawn closer to the light of understanding, to become closer to God through understanding the energies of the heavens.

A divine plan was instrumented which would enable human beings to wake up to their spiritual nature and their spiritual history, should they be willing to commit to this path of higher evolution.

The gods of light also knew that the tool, astrology, would go through many dark periods when human's egos would become stronger than their spiritual values. They also knew that humans on Earth would reach a point where they had the ability to destroy themselves and the planet. They also knew that many humans would join forces with the darker energies and so go into denial of their rightful spiritual heritage.

However, they also knew that the time would come when many individuals would feel a stirring inside themselves, a desire to know and understand more, a desire to evolve back to their spiritual home – to be at one with their Creator, with God.

They knew this desire would turn into a longing, a deep need rising from hidden places in their soul, and so the science of astrology would again come to the forefront of societal thinking.

The gods of light left a legacy.

And so it was that planet Earth once again became the playground of the galaxies. Once again Earth became the Garden of Eden, as it was when the Divine Creator God breathed it into existence at the beginning of time.

the visitors

When the world was young and humans felt differently to what they do now, Mother Earth was happy and she rejoiced with the people. She responded to their care for her.

The people used to give thanks to Mother Earth every day. They would give thanks to the Sun for shining so brightly and filling their lives with such unconditional love in the form of life force energy, warmth and light.

They praised Mother Earth for the abundance of food she provided – for the seasons, those times when food needed to rest and germinate in the ground and those times when the plants would grow strong and produce fruit, flowers, nuts and berries.

These simple people loved and respected their planet and the energy from the Sun. They understood and respected the Moon, as they knew she brought about the changes in the tides. These people honoured all life forms believing all were created as a spark of God and all were to be respected as equal.

All was harmonious on the surface of planet Earth. All was harmonious internally within Mother Earth.

There were no volcanoes erupting, no violent storms, and no tidal waves. All was in harmony with natural law.

Then, one day, out of the blue, fleets of space ships appeared. The simple people on Earth looked at these flying things in the sky with both awe and apprehension. Apprehension because they felt their simple harmonious way of life was about to change, suddenly and irrevocably.

There were hundreds and hundreds of space ships – they hovered all around the populated areas of the planet, and then, as if by magic, beings descended on a light ladder that opened up from the belly of each space ship. These beings were tall, masterful, proud and strong. They were far more advanced technologically than Earth humans.

The people waited, quietly, watching in awe at the sight unfolding in front of their eyes.

The visitors landed where there was raised ground so that they appeared even larger. They towered over the people.

The space visitors spoke to the people, gently and lovingly. They said they didn't want to harm the human inhabitants of Earth. They were simply on a fact-finding mission and were eager to help the people on Earth should humans so desire.

They told of the star system that was their home. They spoke of the love they felt for it and how they honoured it as a special part of God's creation and how pleased they were to see people on Earth honouring their planet in the same way

These beings spoke with such love, warmth,

openness and honesty that the people of Earth immediately welcomed them. Everyone relaxed and began to enjoy the visit of the space people.

The beings from space offered to stay and teach humans simple techniques – ways to improve their life. They taught them how to feel with their hands if a fruit or vegetable was ready to be eaten. They brought with them many seeds from their own star system and showed humans how to plant and grow the seeds so they would produce the best results.

They showed them how to build dwellings out of natural stone and they taught them how to construct implements to help them work the soil. These beings from outer space were honoured and loved by the people on planet Earth. The people felt blessed to have them as their friends and teachers.

The day came when the space visitors were to leave Earth. They had enjoyed their stay. They felt they had contributed to the evolution of the people on Earth. They had gathered data and statistics for their own records as was their mission.

All people benefited from the intermingling. It was a win-win situation for all concerned.

Harmony and balance continued to reign on planet Earth for many centuries. The humans had learned well from their friends from outer space.

Mother Earth was pleased and she rested peacefully. All was well on the planet.

Patricia

It was a long time ago when Patricia first discovered she felt differently about most things to other people. It seemed as if she was from another place. She felt quite alienated from her family and peers and didn't seem to fit in somehow.

At first this had disturbed her but she soon accepted it as a fact of life. She spent a lot of time reading, especially adventure books and philosophical books. She was endeavouring to reach an understanding as to why she felt so foreign in her surroundings.

She found that being in nature helped her quite a lot and she loved to study the animals and birds of the forest. She watched their behaviour, their patterns, and was very intrigued with the way they lived their lives.

As she grew older and experienced many unusual situations she developed a greater knowledge of her origins. Often, when she was reading, her body would react to something in the book. Her body seemed to identify with what she was reading. She began to observe her body as a detached watcher and grew to understand it deeply. She realised that her body contained knowledge – like memories – and these were activated at certain times.

She realised that her body would react when she had a thought that was negative. She began to write down all these observations and after a year or so all the notes she had made began to formulate into a cohesive pattern.

She found that by fully understanding the messages her body was giving her, and by acting on the messages, she was able to maintain her body in a perfect state of health. She understood on some level that she had been involved in natural healing before as the knowledge she was uncovering and bringing into her conscious awareness had been stored somewhere in her being – she had simply not been conscious about it.

Patricia was really excited by all this revelation but found it difficult to communicate her knowledge to others as they looked at her as if she were not quite sane. She had always felt different anyway, so this didn't bother her.

She decided to write a book about her experiences and her findings, hoping that the information would be of benefit to those people who were more in tune with their bodies.

She wrote the book very simply, starting at the beginning with the explanation of how she had always felt different and then going on to explain the process of discovery. She felt uplifted and joyful when writing her experiences, as she knew they would be of benefit to others who felt the same way as she did.

The book was published and was successful and

Patricia had many letters and phone calls from people all over the country who had experienced similar things to her. Great friendships developed due to the common bond that brought them together.

At long last Patricia felt at home and comfortable among her peers. She had found a group of people who shared her ideas and knowledge. She didn't feel alienated any more.

Jack and Dennis

It was a fine sunny day when Jack and Dennis went for a walk. They were teenage boys living in a busy, dirty city and they were bored. They decided to go to some other friends' homes and then, as a group, work off their energy in some way.

The group of five boys was now ready for action – they were up to mischief. They felt like being daring. Each one individually would not consider doing anything mischievous or naughty, but the group energy was such that they felt like invincible warriors and ready to attack the world.

They were all drug users and liked the feelings the drugs gave them. They didn't have to face their own sad selves when on the drugs; they could escape into a dreamworld, one that was full of bright colours and strange images. They laughed together and told each other of the strange trips they were having.

An old lady came walking by and the boys could see her through their strange vision as being someone weak and ineffectual. The drugs made them feel strong and wild, so they decided to play a game with the old lady.

They tripped her over and then sat on her and took

her bag away. She had a little money so they pocketed that.

They then felt power surging forth within them as they sat on top of her. Their maleness, their sexuality, began to arise and they felt stronger and stronger. They began breathing heavily, and great urges welled up inside of them.

They wanted to be superior, to be dominant, to be powerful over the weak old lady. They didn't see her for what she was any more, only that she represented something that they wanted to attack and attack.

All their feelings of frustration, aggression, bravado, arose within them – they egged each other on.

They tore into the old woman with their raging hot piercing penises. They gang raped her. They bashed and mutilated her body and her face with stones and a knife that one of them was carrying. They used their inner frustration, their boredom, to attack, abuse, rape and kill an innocent defenceless old woman.

They were laughing, joking, using obscene language, and dancing around waving their weapons for all to see. They felt invincible. It was a moment of black, horrible power.

A police siren sounded, which brought the boys a little into present time. However, they couldn't see their situation clearly. They were still in a cloudy mist of illusion and fantasy.

They were bundled into the police van and taken to the police station for questioning and still they didn't realise their offence. The drugs were still operating in their bodies.

The police then threw them all into a cell for the

rest of the day and night knowing it would take that long for the boys to recover.

Early the next morning each of the boys began to wake up – wake up to the dawning of a new day, and also to wake up to the events of the day before and their part in it. Jack and Dennis remembered that they were the ones that started out full of life and mischief. They were the ringleaders that had coaxed the others into the drug taking and now they would have to face the consequences of their actions.

There was no one to blame. They had done this terrible act of destruction and cruelty all because they were bored, frustrated and feeling unfulfilled in their lives.

A deep hollow developed in their hearts – a great feeling of overwhelming guilt and remorse. The feeling hit them like a thunderbolt. They would now have to live their entire lives carrying these feelings.

As time went by and their prison sentence was more than half way over the feelings of guilt and remorse still persisted. However, another feeling began to emerge – one of compassion. They had been reaching out for understanding of themselves by reading many of the books in the prison library, and by being counselled by various spiritual people; ministers, priests and spiritualists.

They began to believe in a Creator – a Divine Being whose spark of light was within them. They found with much prayer and meditation the deep hole that was in their hearts was filling in – with light.

The time for release from prison was imminent. They were now middle-aged men – much wiser now.

They offered their services to the drug rehabilitation centres. They now had a mission and purpose in their lives. They wanted to save young people from falling into the same trap they had. They wanted to prevent human destruction by other humans. They believed that if they could save lives by their actions they would be able to leave the planet in a more peaceful state.

They allowed their newfound spiritual practices and spiritual guidance to direct them in their lives.

Their highs now came through loving service. The pain and suffering they had caused could never be wiped from their memories. However, their loving deeds atoned in some small way for the misdemeanours of their youth.

Because they had actually been the perpetrators of a horrendous crime whilst under the influence of drugs and were now teaching others the inherent dangers of drug taking, they were well received at all the meetings they attended.

They were able to graphically describe the feelings that arose within them at the time of the crime and the feelings of remorse, guilt, self-hatred and disgust that occurred afterwards.

All those who attended the meetings were moved by the sincerity of the men. Jack and Dennis did save many young lives.

samantha

A long time ago in a far distant land lived a young girl whose name was Samantha. She was called Sammy. Because she was such a tomboy she was often confused herself as to whether she was a boy or a girl. It wasn't until she was nearly a teenager that she found out the physical difference between girls and boys. She was quite perplexed when she discovered this information and quite disappointed also because she had always felt so comfortable playing with other boys.

Samantha lived in a country where not every child attended school. She was one of the children who did not. Her parents were unable to afford to send her to school to learn. They believed that her brother needed to go to school but not Samantha. This was because she was a girl and girls were meant to stay at home and cook and look after the other children in the family. After they had grown up they were expected to marry and look after their husband.

Sammy, who was a free spirit, felt hemmed in by this scenario. She believed that she was just as good as a boy and was able to do all the things that boys could do, so she believed she was entitled to go to school.

This passion for learning became so great that she decided to dress up as a boy and go off to school each day. She lied to her parents about where she was going and she made sure that she had done all her household chores before she left for school. She also made sure she went to a school in a different neighbourhood so that she wouldn't be known. She used to chop wood for the neighbours in order to make enough money to pay for her school fees.

She was so determined to learn. As you can imagine, she was very quick to understand all that the teachers were teaching. She became a very clever student. She was able to do this for three years but then her mother had another baby and Samantha was expected to look after the new baby. Samantha's freedom was curtailed.

Her life became a drudgery. Her mother was weakened by the birth of the new baby so Samantha had to be nurse, cook, and clean for her mother, as well as look after the baby and attend to his needs.

Samantha was happy to help for a while but then she began to feel resentful, bitter and angry inside. She buried all these emotions. She began to get very depressed, sullen and unresponsive to her family. All her love of life and learning had eroded.

She lived her life like a robot, doing what had to be done, not caring anymore about herself, her interests, and her passion for learning. She felt trapped, helpless, and began then to feel worthless. She felt she was only good enough to be a slave or a servant around the house. This time in her life was a very dark period. She became dark – all the light left her.

One day, when she was taking her young brother for a walk, she was stopped by the teacher she had had when at school. This teacher was so happy to see her but was quite confused, as he had always believed Samantha to be a boy.

Samantha told the teacher her story and what had happened to her since her happy school days. Her teacher was very saddened by her story and the state of darkness she was in. He asked her if she still wanted to learn. Because she was so unresponsive and depressed and couldn't see how that could ever be again she told him she really didn't care anymore.

The teacher then said that it was up to her. If she were able to pull herself up and out of her darkness herself and if she wanted to do this enough, then it would happen. She had to do the work. She had to gather her own inner strength. She had to learn how to express her buried emotions in a responsible way so as not to hurt others and when she was able to do this she would feel much lighter.

He said he would be willing to teach her again after he had finished school each day. He told her that she had to do her bit by being honest to her parents by telling them the whole story, by being willing to face the consequences and then to also tell them of her longing to learn more. When she could do this with love rather than with resentment and bitterness she could then become his pupil again.

A glimmer of light, of hope, entered Samantha's being. For the first time in many years she experienced a slight tinge of excitement. She knew it would be very hard for her to face her parents to tell them her story and her deepest feelings, but she also knew it was the only thing to do if she wanted to break out of her present life, which she felt was like a prison to her.

Because she could write, she decided to write down all her feelings. She found that this helped make things clearer in her head. She found herself chopping wood again and this helped clear some of the anger out of her body. She pretended the wood was her parent's beliefs and she was able to smash them in two. She was beginning to feel stronger and clearer in her thoughts.

She decided to talk to her mother first and to tell her the story. She gathered courage, first by walking with her younger brother outside in the fresh air and getting herself prepared.

She spoke lovingly to her mother, from her heart, expressing all the joy she had experienced when learning and how she had felt resentful and angry when her learning had been curtailed.

She told her mother how much she loved her and her younger brother and how she would be able to still help them but she wanted some time to go to the teacher so that she could continue learning.

Because Samantha had spoken her deepest truth and was taking responsibility for her feelings and was not making her mother wrong, her mother listened and felt Samantha's passion for learning. She felt Samantha's joy. She felt her heart speak. She was moved. She said she would support her and asked her to speak to her father that evening.

Again Samantha needed to gather her inner

strength, her courage, to face her father. She realised how important it was to speak from her heart simply and lovingly without any dark feelings arising. She felt love and respect for her father and the struggles he had to raise his family. She expressed this to him and told him her story. She said she still wanted to help around the house but would be able to do it more joyfully and lovingly if her needs were met. As she continued to express herself from her heart she could feel herself becoming calmer, more peaceful, lighter.

Her father also felt her words deep within him. He loved her and realised how she had changed from the active, joyful, playful tomboy to the sullen, sad, and depressed girl.

He told her that if she could still do all the chores around the house she could go off each day for one and a half hours in order to learn from the teacher.

Samantha was overjoyed. She realised that it takes courage to face inner dragons, inner fears. It takes courage to confront those in authority. It takes courage to confront and express what is truly inside a heart and if that courage can be accessed and utilised, then all sorts of exciting things can happen. Joy results from being in the light of truth.

Samantha now had a wonderful life to look forward to. She also felt she wanted to teach her younger brother all that she was learning. Life was becoming exciting again.

David

It was a long time ago when David realised he was special. He understood he had special gifts and talents that others did not seem to have. He could see things with his inner eye that others seemed not to be able to see. He could sense and feel situations and had an inner knowing about the way events would manifest in his life. He was attuned to the inner worlds.

One day his mother asked him to go on a message for her. She wanted him to visit his Aunt and take her a special gift; something David's mother had made. David willingly agreed to deliver the gift even though it meant walking for quite some distance away from his home. He eagerly set out on his journey knowing that something out of the ordinary was going to happen to him. He could sense it.

As he was drawing near to his Aunt's home his attention was drawn to a bright light that appeared in the sky. The light grew brighter and brighter as he approached his destination. It seemed to hover over the roof of his aunt's house.

He left the parcel at his Aunt's front door and walked around to her back yard to see if he could see the source of the light more clearly.

The brightness intensified. It seemed to be a beam of light coming from the heavens and radiating the back garden. He stepped into the beam and felt himself merging with the light. He felt himself being transported up the beam of light quite easily and comfortably. He felt safe and happy.

He entered some kind of a craft. It felt solid but somehow he sensed it was more light than matter. He felt himself propelled into a space where everything glowed golden. He felt he was glowing with golden light.

He then saw an angelic being – a female with much love emanating from her. She seemed so beautiful, glowing with such radiance that David felt a great surge of emotion rush through his heart.

Her name was Gabrielle. She was like a guardian angel, beaming to him such love and compassion. She beckoned him to follow her into another part of the craft. He bathed in her golden aura – it enveloped him as he walked behind her. She entered a space that seemed to be a soft clear pink. She bade him enter. He felt the colour wash all over him, filling his whole being with warmth and love.

Gabrielle gave him a gift – a special symbol that he was to keep – a gift from a heavenly being that he was to hold sacred within his heart. The gift was a golden cup – a grail – a vessel symbolising the fullness of his soul.

He thanked Gabrielle for her gift and for such a wonderful experience. She then said to him, "Be still and know thou art God." She said this three times.

David replied, "I am God," and said this three times.

The ritual was complete. David had been initiated into a high level of spiritual experience.

He knew great trust and faith were being placed in him and he knew he had a special task, or role to play in his life on Earth. He knew he would need to have integrity within himself at all times in order to fulfil his task. He felt honoured to be the recipient of such a great gift.

He found himself back on the lawn of his Aunt's garden and rested there for sometime allowing his experiences of the higher realms to integrate within him.

He understood his path would reveal itself when the time was right. He knew he would be ready to walk that path when it was presented to him. He was willing and committed to that journey wherever it was to take him. He needed only to be aware of the signs, the omens, and listen to his heart and he would be guided all along the way.

He was well content.

Polly's Research

Polly had many friends who loved and supported her. She could always count on their counsel whenever she needed guidance. She had the ability to listen to what they had to say and then be able to discern what felt applicable to her own situation. She understood their advice was based on their own perceptions. She knew there were many ways of perceiving reality.

Polly was a scientist, delving deep into the realms of medical research. She loved her work but often felt very frustrated at her inability to pin point the causes of illness. Often she felt she had nearly solved the problem only to find herself back at the beginning again. It was as if there was a missing link which modern research didn't seem to grasp.

She decided to do her own field of study, totally divorced from her formal training. She cared so much about healing people and realised she couldn't do it to her capacity based on the mindset of formal modern medicine.

She pondered the problem, allowing her rational, logical mind a space to rest whilst consciously enlisting the aid of her intuitive mind.

Polly practiced many spiritual rituals and meditation was one of them. She had found it was a tremendous relaxing aid to her when she was studying for all her exams and had made it a regular practice. She would often go out into her garden and sit under the mango tree with her back resting against the trunk. She would consciously relax her body through deep breathing exercises and focus on all the different parts of her body. She would then call in her spirit guides and ask them for guidance.

One morning during her meditation ritual she had an impression form in her mind of some ancient text. She became excited about this message as she intuitively recognised that this was in some way connected to her work dilemma.

She decided to go the local library and asked her guides to direct her to just the right book that would help her to understand her problem. The library was huge and she found herself in a section she had never even looked at before. She felt excitement welling up inside of her.

One book seemed to be jumping out at her. It seemed to be prominent in its position on the shelf even though it wasn't a large book. She reached up to take it from the shelf when it seemed to fall into her hands. It felt right. She didn't even look at the title because she knew she was being guided to take this particular book home with her.

She turned the book over and saw that it was a book on energy. It appeared to describe how energy from the cosmos works in all living things and how this energy can be felt, monitored and calculated.

Her heart was beating rapidly. She knew she was on to something very deep and profound. She also felt a sense of responsibility as she knew her life would change from the reading, integration and application of the information.

She took the book home and studied it carefully. It was a book on astrology with a particular section on medical astrology. The book explained how astrology was an ancient science that had been tested and researched for many thousands of years.

The section on medical astrology had many case histories and these really excited her as she could correlate them with her own research. She knew she had made a monumental discovery, one that would benefit many people.

She felt such a surge of energy inside of her as she committed to the study of this science of cosmic energy. She knew it would aid her in getting to the causes of illness in humans.

Because Polly had an open and inquiring mind and was willing to trust her inner guidance she was able to be a catalyst and a pioneer in a field of science that seemed obscure to so many.

Polly's research helped to heal millions of people from debilitating illnesses. She felt very fulfilled with her work and lived a prosperous and very healthy life. She was also able to help her friends with their emotional, mental and physical problems and taught them how to tune into their own inner guidance through training themselves to relax and be receptive to intuitive impressions.

Her heart-felt intention to source the causes of

illness was energy that she put out to the cosmos. The manifestation of this intention and her commitment took her on a path of discovery that changed her life, and the lives of many others, for the better.

Evolution on Earth

A long, long time ago when the Earth was young, many unusual species of animals roamed her surface. There were huge dinosaurs of many different kinds. These animals played a part in the evolution of the human race.

When it was time for man to become human the dinosaurs chose to leave the planet. They left it in good condition.

Humans were impulsed by stellar beings to begin the process of evolution. Their brainpower was extremely limited. They had instinctual habits but were not able to reason with their intellect. This function took a long time to develop.

Many aeons ago, a race of star beings came to Planet Earth to assist humans to evolve. They brought with them advanced technology. They intermingled with humans and taught them how to apply themselves to simple tasks and how to reason. Humans were not quick to learn and it took many hundreds of years to bring any marked level of evolvement.

The stellar beings decided then to interbreed with humans. This way, humans would evolve much more quickly. Hybrid humans were born with a mixture of human and stellar genes.

The human race began to evolve at a much faster rate. Progress was made in all avenues of life – mental, practical, and spiritual. Humankind was adapting and changing. They admired and respected their stellar brothers and sisters.

The time came for the stellar beings to leave Earth – to let their students fend for themselves. They had been master teachers and it was now up to the students to continue to evolve unaided. There was much sorrow on Earth as the space visitors left. They had become part of Earthly life and humans were afraid they might not be able to manage without their friends.

Time passed – centuries passed, and then one day a spacecraft was noticed, hovering around temple structures. Some people went into fear, but most people felt memories stirring within them – memories of another time when the space visitors lived amongst them.

The spacecraft landed. Many beings descended and they were greeted with both apprehension and curiosity. However, it soon became apparent that these beings were smarter, more intelligent and much more advanced than those humans on Earth. The space visitors wanted control of some of Earth's resources, especially gold. There was little gold where they came from and these beings needed it for their health and the health of their planet.

They were like gods to the humans and expected to be treated this way. These beings were not totally evil – they just wanted control of the humans who were around them and control of Earth's resources.

As time went by some of these gods sexually interacted with humans and another hybrid developed. The genetic mix was unusual as the space visitors had no emotional body – their make up was more metallic and so they were unfeeling and unemotional. However, they found that when in the act of sexual intercourse strange energies soared through them.

When it was time to leave the planet and return to their own home far away in space, they carried with them the memories of their sexual encounters with humans. They also carried with them the knowledge of how to use energy to impulse humans into doing their bidding.

They chose to continue this practice. They impulse, via thought waves, humans who are hybrid, to do things for them which is always to do with power and manipulation of some kind. These space beings are able to control humans on Earth through impulsing them to think dark thoughts and to do dark deeds.

Those humans that follow these impulses do so because they want to feel powerful in some way. They want to have power over people by controlling the media or the government and the financial institutions. They get their pay-off in monetary rewards and the feelings of power this engenders within them.

It is time for planet Earth to evolve to a higher level – a level where power over others and inappropriate abuse of resources will not be tolerated. All dark motives such as greed will be transformed.

The space visitors who played their game so well now realise they have created a monster that could easily destroy itself. They realise they have gone too far. Their selfish push for power, control and domination has almost resulted in the destruction of Earth.

New light needs to enter the consciousness of humans. A re-generation needs to occur – all the weeds of the past need to be pulled out.

At this time in human evolution there are many beings from other planets and star systems endeavouring to break through our barriers of consciousness. Most of them are committed to healing Planet Earth as best they can. These beings come to aid humans from a loving place. They do not want power over the people. They encourage humans to come into balance through love.

The evolution on Earth will proceed. Love and Light will overtake power, control and greed.

GARY

It was a cold, damp morning and Gary huddled into the blankets not wanting to get up and face his day. He had many problems at his work place and always felt agitated and stressed about confronting the issues.

He nestled down into his bed, unconsciously breathing deeply. He found himself relaxing and feeling calmer than he had done for some time. He wondered how he could maintain this feeling. If felt good – peaceful somehow. He pondered this for sometime and then accepted that it was really his responsibility to continue to feel this way. No other person could do it for him. It was his body and only he knew how his own body worked.

As he continued lying in bed he found himself becoming conscious of his deep breathing and became aware that this seemed to relax him. He then remembered he had read somewhere how many people practice conscious deep breathing exercises, focusing on each individual part of their body as a means of relaxing tension, so he decided to do this practice.

He had some success although it took mind

discipline to focus on each body part. He could, however, feel less tension in his body so knew it was working to some extent.

Gary then committed to follow a course of action whereby he would practice this method of relaxation every day, especially just before he had to confront uncomfortable situations at his work.

He tried his new found relaxation technique before his meetings that day and found it required a great deal of will, discipline and effort to focus and concentrate on his breathing. He discovered that when he was able to do so his sessions always flowed more smoothly and with a lot less friction and stress. He knew this was good for his health. It was as if the calmer energy he was putting out attracted the same calmer energy to him.

Gary was now learning how to be responsible for his own body and learning to feel the difference between feeling stressed and agitated and feeling calm and centred. He decided to pursue this matter further and only a few hours after he had made this decision he saw a notice on the board at work advising of a yoga class commencing the following week. It was to be conducted one hour before scheduled work time. Gary was intrigued by this – quite curious – as it seemed to be quite coincidental to his earlier decision.

He decided to follow this trail so committed to attend the class, at least for a few mornings, just to see how he felt.

At first he felt uncomfortable with the class as the concepts were foreign to him. However, he could feel his body respond to the exercises and he especially appreciated the relaxation exercises at the end of the class.

After a few classes he found that he was relaxing a little more during the day and his body was not so tight. His mind also seemed more focused. His worries didn't seem so important any more and he was developing a different perspective on his life. He was placing more value on his body and his health than he had ever done before and he realised this was definitely an improvement to his life style.

He then found he looked forward to his yoga classes each morning and was always eager to get out of bed early to begin his day.

Gary's health and perception of life kept on changing for the better as he became more conscious of his own energy levels. He learned to pace himself and to become more detached and not react emotionally to confronting situations. He realised that it was the emotional stress that caused a lot of imbalances in his body.

He also learned to train his mind to think more positive thoughts as he grew to understand that his negative thoughts drew difficult situations to him.

Gary was always very grateful to his own inner guidance for directing him on his path towards inner harmony and improved health. He became an example to his staff, work associates and family and they too benefited from his experiences.

Communing with nature spirits

Once upon a time, when the Earth was young, fairies, elves and gnomes used to be visible to all humans.

These delightful nature spirits worked each day to produce the plants and the minerals on Mother Earth. Their energy helped to form the colours of the plants and flowers and the structure of the minerals. Humans were grateful to the nature spirits for the role they played in co-creating the paradise that was Earth.

Humans had a highly developed intuitive function at this time. Their brow chakra, or third eye, was open and they used their sixth sense naturally and easily.

They could also see and commune with the 'mer' people; those water beings that lived in the sea. They often had parties together, each respecting the other's role in creation, each accepting the other's right to be.

As time progressed and humans evolved to the use of their left brain faculties, that area of the brain that deals with rational, logical thought, they began to question that which they were seeing with their sixth sense. As they began to question they began to doubt. When they started doubting, they lost their trust and it appeared as if the nature spirits gradually died out.

Humans, as a mass, began to deny the existence of these nature spirits and water beings. They closed down a part of themselves that had functioned so successfully for millions of years.

There are a few people on planet Earth now who have this second sight – who are able to see our friends and co-creators from other dimensions. These people do not deny their visions. They trust what they are seeing and know it to be true for them.

Many young children also have the sight and many play happily for hours with their friends from the nature kingdoms. Once again people are beginning to wake up to themselves – to access that part of them that they allowed to atrophy. The opening is occurring; the awakening is gathering momentum.

Our friends and co-creators from the plant and mineral kingdoms are waiting to work in co-operation with us once more. We need only to open ourselves up to their existence. They are waiting eagerly for humans to again open up their intuitive right brain function and to see the big picture of creation. They want humans to co-create consciously with them so that Mother Earth can be again restored to the paradise that she once was, so long ago.

power

A long time ago, when the Earth was younger, humans lived in very advanced civilisations. They had much knowledge. They were more developed technologically than they are now.

There were two distinct groups of people. Those who were into power trips and those that followed natural spiritual laws. Those that were into power trips were very like the majority on Earth today, except they had more knowledge than Earthlings today. They sought power over people and their environment for their own ends. They were selfish, egotistical, arrogant and materialistic. They always wanted bigger and better, and more and more. They cared little for nature and their whole focus was on themselves and what they could get. They wanted power over their world, so they build weapons that would have the capacity to generate so much power that others would fear them. They used Earth crystals and synthetic crystals as their source of power.

The other group of people were living their lives according to natural and spiritual laws. They were aware of the gigantic power struggle that was going on in the hearts and minds of the others and they felt saddened by the obsessive, compulsive attempts at control.

These spiritual people were also seers – they could see with their inner vision that the power-hungry moguls would blow themselves and all of their civilisation out of existence, so they made preparations for departure.

The power-hungry scientists created a massive, incredibly huge crystal, which they kept inside a top security building. Only a few select people were allowed into this building. The scientists were experimenting with the crystal. They wanted to find out just how much power it did actually contain.

The spiritual people, who lived according to natural law, could read the omens in the skies. They could see when the energies of the heavens would be beaming down specific frequencies that could result in men behaving very destructively through their lack of understanding of the planetary forces. They chose to remove themselves from the country. They left their country of birth *en masse* and chose to begin a new life in a different place.

Many of them went to Egypt and many to the Americas.

The scientists began their experiments. The power surges not only went up through the top of the crystal into the atmosphere but also went down into the belly of Mother Earth causing shock waves. These shock waves created huge fissures in the Earth. The atmosphere was pierced, the seas boiled up, volcanoes erupted and tidal waves decimated the cities. All the buildings crumbled.

The Earth opened up her belly and swallowed the civilisation. She then covered it with water.

The abuse of power inside the hearts and minds of humans had resulted in the total annihilation of an entire civilisation.

Those humans with love in their hearts were free to build a new civilisation based on natural, spiritual laws rather than man-made laws.

King Arthur

It was a long, long time ago when Arthur was king in a green and gentle land. Arthur was loved by his subjects and his family. He was an adventurous king and believed in applying natural law to his every day life. His kingdom flourished.

One day a stranger appeared at King Arthur's castle. This stranger seemed quite old because he had a long white beard. However, he had bright, twinkling, mischievous eyes, certainly not the eyes of an old man.

Arthur was intrigued by this man so invited him into the castle. The man, we shall call him Merlin, was a wizard. He was a wise one who understood the natural laws of the Universe and knew how to work with them to produce what seemed to be magic. He worked for the good of humanity. He was not into manipulative black magic.

The king was fascinated with Merlin and asked him to stay in the castle for some time. He gave him large quarters – a whole wing in the castle. He had a bedroom, a sitting room and a workroom.

Arthur wondered at this strange change to his life and wondered about the outcome. He knew nothing ever happens in life without reason, and that there are no coincidences, so he was content to wait and watch whatever game was about to be played.

Arthur spent a great deal of time with Merlin and Merlin taught him much. Merlin had appeared in Arthur's life at a crucial time in his evolutionary development. It had been time for him to move forward in his understanding of life, so the teacher had appeared. Arthur was astute enough to be aware of this.

As time went by Arthur became adept at 'magic'. He was able to use the universal energies to work through him in such a way that he could shape shift. He could still physically be in the castle, but also be seen in other places. Sometimes, he shape shifted into the form of an animal just to see what it felt like. These practices required much concentration and mind control and Arthur often made mistakes. Merlin was always there to help him out, often laughing at the king's antics.

Merlin had the capacity to heal people through tuning into their energy inside of them. He could follow the current into the organs of the body and see what needed to be done to affect healing. Usually, the cause was some incident or traumatic event that had left an energetic imprint or a blockage in the body. Merlin could see the incident and how the person had felt at the time and the thoughtform that had formed, and was able to tell the person about it and then, if the person was willing to let the old thoughtform and feeling go, a healing would take place.

Merlin helped to move Arthur up the evolutionary ladder into a state of knowing and understanding more about himself and how he carried within him a spark of the Divine energy and how he too could be a co-creator of his world, just as God was a creator.

As the king matured and looked back on his life he could see how Merlin had appeared at just the right time for him to grow and expand in conscious understanding of himself and his world.

He gave thanks to the Divine Creator, the spark of God that was inside of him, for the blessing of Merlin's presence in his life.

MARY

It was a long time ago when Mary realised she was special and different from other people. She always felt alienated when in the company of others. She experienced a sense of being separate – not one of the gang. She realised that others felt a sense of connection, of belonging, but she felt such a loner. She didn't understand why this was, but understood it was the case.

She chose to spend much time alone as she felt more comfortable with her own company. She felt more peaceful.

One day when Mary was totally focussed on her reading she experienced a strange sensation. She felt as if she was part of the story. She felt she knew what the outcome of the story would be. It seemed to her that she had lived this story in another time. It seemed so real to her.

The story ended exactly as she knew it would. This caused her to think deeply on this. She felt quite certain she had lived this story herself. She knew this in the inner most part of her being. She understood then that in order to have experienced it she must have lived it in another place and another time. This had her thinking about other lives. She then understood quite clearly that the 'she' who had lived before was still the 'she' that was living now – however, the body was different. This made Mary realise that the 'she' can have many lives, many experiences in different dimensions of time and space. The 'she' seemed as if it could go on forever, gathering and dropping new bodies along the journey.

Mary was highly intrigued by this reasoning and she knew she had uncovered a deep truth about life. She realised that the 'she' that went on to different lives was more in spirit form which took on a body of matter for each different incarnation.

Mary then pondered as to the meaning and purpose of all of this. There must be a reason this is so. Mary felt really excited at all these revelations that she was having and wanted to unfold the rest of the story.

She understood the 'she' that carried through the incarnations was a spirit with a consciousness and therefore was made up of energetic particles. The consciousness of the 'she' also had a memory – some kind of record-storing system and that this 'she' could access all the records if 'she' chose to do so.

Mary then understood that in order for this to take place a different level, or band, of consciousness needed to be experienced. She decided to practice at achieving this different state, firstly by learning to focus on one thing really intensely whilst at the same time calming her emotional nature and stilling any mind chatter. This took practice and patience. However, Mary's desire to understand more kept her on this path.

When she had mastered this higher vibrational state she then allowed her mind to become receptive.

Whilst engaging in this meditative procedure she always made sure she sent a prayer to God, or her Guardian Angel, to protect her energy field from any darker energies that might be lurking around. She somehow knew it was important to do this.

Sometimes, when in this altered state, she was able to receive messages that were always uplifting, encouraging and pertinent for her and sometimes she had visions of herself in situations, which were taking place in another time and another space.

She began to have the understanding that somehow all of us are complex beings, able to operate on many different levels of experience and that somehow everyone is connected by threads of energy.

As Mary was unravelling this mystery of existence she found herself more at ease with others now – she was feeling more peaceful within herself. This seemed to be a wonderful by-product of her deeper understanding and of the meditative procedures she was involved in each day.

Mary decided she would like to help others to understand life from a larger perspective should they be interested in learning from her. She started holding classes and many people were drawn to them, just like a magnet draws iron filings to it. Mary had become magnetic, attracting others who also wanted to uncover some of life's mysteries.

Mary never felt alienated or separated again. She had made herself whole through discovering her real true self that had been hidden under the veil of the personality self. She found her spirit connection to God and felt whole and complete because of this.

mother earth

A very long time ago, when the Earth was young, human beings lived a very peaceful, fulfilled and contented life. All their needs were met. They had natural shelter, plenty of food and the sun warmed their bodies. Temperatures were even – there was no great distortion or range of extremes. That happened much later.

Human beings lived in harmony with all of nature. All were considered equal. All had their place in the great scheme of things. All were respected for the roles they played.

Trees and plants were honoured as valuable members of society. Birds and insects were honoured and valued for the contribution they made. Animals were honoured, as were the creatures of the sea.

Mother Nature was pleased. Earth was honoured and worshipped. Gratitude was expressed daily for the bounty she produced.

All lived in harmony with the Divine Plan. The Creator was pleased with the way its creation was manifesting.

All was created in the likeness of God – that is, all with a spark of Divine energy. Each species, human, plant, animal, insect, fish all were created from the same stuff – the energy that was within them all is the same as the energy of God.

God then had an idea – another one. This idea was that all life needed to experience, to learn to feel many different things. God understood that living in absolute harmony was blissful, however, there was very little growth or evolution occurring.

God wanted to expand, grow and become – so the idea was that all parts of Her/Him were to expand, grow and become even more evolved. It was the way to go. If all parts within Her/Him could expand and grow then the energy that was God the Creator could also expand, grow and evolve.

This idea pleased the Divine Creator. The thought-form was sent out from the mind of God to the ethers. God felt excitement at the prospect of a change of status quo occurring. God didn't know what the humans would do with the energy of change. Because they were allowed free will, they were free to choose their path themselves.

All God knew for certain was that change would take place and the changes would result in expansion and growth of humans and thus evolution would occur.

God waited.

Humans were slow to pick up on God's idea. They were used to being instinctual and their ways were quite fixed. They didn't want to change. They liked being in their comfort zone – it felt safe and secure.

Then one day a strange sight appeared. What appeared to be strange flying things, littered the sky.

There were so many of these things that looked like huge, unusual birds, and they hovered over the people.

The people were not afraid, as they were not used to that emotion, however they were curious. They watched and waited.

Ladders of light seemed to appear from the belly of the flying things and human-like people descended. They were tall, seemed masterful and were obviously more highly evolved than humans on Earth. They raised their hands in a peaceful gesture and the people encircled them wanting to touch the unusual visitors from the sky.

The visitors communicated telepathically to the inhabitants, telling them they had come to Earth specifically to teach humans about themselves, about natural law, and to assist their evolution. They told how they had felt impulsed to come, through promptings by the Divine Creator. They said the reason for life on Earth and on other planets and star systems was for all living things to evolve, through experiencing and feeling, to a higher understanding of self. That, as all living things evolved and expanded their conscious understanding, so too did God, the Divine Creator expand and evolve as well.

The space visitors said it was time for Earthlings to develop into more conscious beings through experiencing a greater variety of emotions, feelings, and experiences. As they were not able to do this as a mass then an outside influence needed to manifest in order for them to move on and up the evolutionary ladder.

"The time has come," the visitors said, "to begin a

new phase of your evolutionary journey. You have been stuck in your old patterns of thought and behaviour for too long. You have become static and dull. We are here to assist you and to serve you. We are here to teach you new ways of thinking and being. We come in loving service. We are willing to teach you our ways of living and our understandings of natural law. You only need to ask us."

The inhabitants of Earth listened with their minds to the words of the visitors. They felt unusual feelings inside of them. They felt stirring in their bodies that they had not experienced before. The visitors were certainly bringing change. It was felt by all.

Some felt their hearts beating. Some felt a queasiness in their stomachs, some felt excitement like electrical currents running through them. They all felt something different.

God smiled. The idea was beginning to be made manifest. God wondered what humans would do with these new feelings and experiences. Would they create for themselves an easy, joyful evolutionary path, or would they create for themselves a path of sadness, negativity, lack and darkness. Whatever they created would be of their own doing.

As time went by the space visitors intermingled with humans. They lovingly taught them many things. They introduced ways to help them select and prepare food. They showed them healing plants. They taught them about the energy from the solar system and how to work with it for the best results.

These space visitors kept to their own kind. They did not choose to interbreed with the humans on

Earth. They simply wanted to pass on information of a practical nature to help aid human development. The visitors loved their holiday on Planet Earth. It was such a beautiful place. They called it the jewel of the galaxy. It seemed to sparkle with such radiant beauty at all times.

Mother Earth was pleased with the visitors' love and admiration so she grew even more beautiful. Her lakes and seas shimmered with light and cleanliness, her forests grew taller and greener and her plants and flowers grew more profusely. Abundance was created. Much love, laughter and joy were felt and experienced by the masses. Harmony prevailed.

Eventually, the space visitors left Earth. They had served the humans on Earth well. They had taught them much and the inhabitants of Earth had been eager students. All benefited from the interchange.

Then, many, many years after the space visitors left, some humans became lazy, feeling it took too much effort to live in accordance with the ways of the space visitors. They began to rebel and to opt out of the community programs the visitors had introduced. They didn't want to do their bit for the community any more. They wanted to do for themselves only. Selfishness was being experienced quite strongly by many people.

These individual thoughtforms collected together to form a mass. The mass of energy became more and more and this mass of thoughtform energy then impregnated itself into the minds of others.

Some who felt this impulse had the mind control and awareness to understand where the thought was coming from and directed it back to its source with love, but most were unconscious and unaware and took the thoughtform into themselves.

As time passed it became apparent that more and more humans were buying into the negative, dark thoughtforms. More and more people rebelled against the communal ways. People became dissatisfied with their lives, they became envious of the freedom they perceived some individuals experienced and they wanted to experience the same thing.

Mother Earth felt the unrest. She wasn't feeling so balanced and peaceful any more. Parts of her began to feel dis-eased.

Aeons passed. Humans now lived unfulfilling lives. They did not experience the peace and joy of living that they once had. Their lives became empty and devoid of meaning. They became more and more robotic.

Mother Earth tried to awaken them by displays of aggression and anger. She started volcanic eruptions. She shuddered and shook in her pain and agony and released her blocked emotions through earthquakes.

She cried huge tears and there were tidal waves. But still humans didn't get the message.

Human living worsened. People did despicable things to each other. They murdered, butchered, raped and denigrated each other and the land that nourished them. They ate each other. They sacrificed young children to appease the gods. They lost all connection to the divine spark of energy that was in their hearts.

A black, dark period was on Earth. There was very little light in the hearts and minds of the people. They were obsessed with power, destruction, lust, envy and greed. They had no time to devote to their children, their families, and their community. Their only focus was that of selfish pursuits – how they could get what other's had – how they could take what they wanted.

Their whole value system was based on getting, rather than giving.

Mother Earth had had enough. The people didn't value her anymore. She was defiled, abused, disregarded and desecrated.

Enough was enough.

She collected all her internal energies, her will, and with intent exhaled deeply. Her waters rose and spilled all over the populated lands. Where there was once land there was now water. She belched and land rose up where there had been water.

A whole civilisation of humans was wiped out. There was no one alive to tell the tale.

She calmed herself and her boiling emotions subsided. The entire face of Mother Earth was transformed, never to be the same again.

She prepared herself for a long period of rest and recuperation. She knew she needed to heal her wounds. She needed the energy of the sun to warm her and give her light.

She rested peacefully.

melody

In ancient Egypt many people lived simple yet meaningful lives. Their days were occupied by ritualistic endeavours. Their beliefs revolved around pleasing the gods. They believed that if the gods were happy then they too would be happy and their lives fulfilling.

Some of the neophytes in the temple began questioning the beliefs of the masses. These neophytes had inquiring minds, they were willing to question, to listen to their intuitive voice and were willing to trust their internal impulses, no matter how strange and unusual this appeared to be. They rebelled against the status quo.

Early one morning, one of the neophytes in the temple received an impulse to watch the sun rise. She was sitting in her room watching the incredibly beautiful scene unfolding in front of her eyes and feeling the grandeur and majesty of creation when she heard a voice speak to her. The voice was coming from inside her head. It wasn't a thought of her own – it was a message coming through her mind.

The neophyte, we shall call her Melody, listened attentively to the message. She trusted herself and didn't question what was coming through her.

The message said, "You are to be the instrument of change. Your role on planet Earth is to light the way so that others may follow. You are to be the lighthouse shining forth into the darkness, illuminating people's minds with a new vision for the future. Follow your impulses, follow your intuition, listen to your heart. We are guiding you in this way."

Melody felt excited yet a little apprehensive with his message and the possible ramifications. However, in her heart of hearts she knew she would follow this path, not knowing where it would lead, simply trusting that all would be well.

Melody loved the stones from Mother Earth. She loved feeling them; she loved looking deeply into their inner realms – she felt deeply connected to the Mineral Kingdom. She was happiest when playing with the rocks and minerals of the Earth.

One day she received a strong impulse to travel to another place that was quite some distance from the temple. Acting on this impulse she found herself in a strange part of the country. People were different and the rocks were different. She was excited and a little apprehensive about what was going to happen.

As she began tuning into the rocks she sensed unusual energy inside her – it was as if a transference of energy was taking place between the rocks and her. She felt electrical impulses in her body that she had never experienced before. She felt as if the consciousness of the rock was trying to get inside her consciousness.

Because she trusted, she allowed the process to

continue, watching and observing herself as she was experiencing.

She could feel small currents of energy flowing through her cells. She felt more awareness, a heightened sense of space, a sensation of merging with all of nature, of becoming one with nature with the rocks around her. She felt like the rock – solid, grounded, contained and yet part of all.

Melody's conscious understanding of herself and her view of the world went through a dramatic change because of this experience. On some deep level of her being a transformation had taken place. She knew there would be many more unusual experiences for her. She knew that she was somehow being prepared for greater things and she understood that it was all part of her destiny. She knew she needed to detach from any outcome and just go along with these unusual impulses whenever they presented themselves to her.

Her life became like a wonderful adventure – a journey into the mysteries of life. Her questioning nature was always seeking clues to the ever-unfolding path. She also knew that her journey of learning would show others how to expand their conscious understanding of life. This is the way she could be the lighthouse.

She was a pioneer, showing by example a new path.

She was well content.

nancy and penny

There was once a young girl whose name was Nancy. Nancy lived in a beautiful country where there were lots of space to play, lots and lots of trees and plants and beautiful weather most of the year.

Nancy loved playing outside in nature. She loved playing barefoot on the grass and frolicking amongst the trees and plants. She was a very happy child and her parents were also very happy. They lived a simple yet very fulfilling and loving life.

In another part of the country lived another girl who was not so fortunate. She lived in a city where there was lots of smoke, smog and very few trees. The people who built the city had chopped down most of the trees to build houses and factories, not realising that the trees were needed to absorb the bad gases and to give out fresh oxygen.

This little girl, we shall call her Penny, often became ill, particularly when the smog was so great that she found herself unable to breath. It seemed like her lungs were full of bad air. She felt suffocated by the horrible smells and fumes. She was a very sensitive girl. Her parents loved her very much and could see that she was suffering by living in this city. They didn't know what to do because both of them had good jobs in the city and were earning very good money.

Penny became really ill and the doctor told her parents that unless she was taken from the polluted city she might die. The parents then realised what their true values were. Penny's life was far more important to them than making money. They were upset with themselves because they hadn't had this understanding before and they hoped it wasn't too late to save Penny's life.

They had no idea where they would go or what would happen when they got to wherever it was. They just knew they had to quickly get Penny away to a healthier environment. They packed up their belongings, put their house on the market and took off for the country and a cleaner environment.

It so happened that they stopped in the part of the country where Nancy lived. They were picnicking in a field under trees when Nancy came running by, barefoot and happy. She stopped to talk to Penny and told her all about her life in the country, about the little village school she attended and about the warmness and kindness of the neighbouring people.

Penny asked her parents if she could live in this wonderful place. She felt very warm and contented here. Nancy told them that there was a house available in the village, just the next place to where she lived, so they all collected the picnic things and went to see the house.

Penny loved the house. She loved the space in the garden. She loved the way the sun shone brightly through the trees. She particularly loved to see the clear blue sky. She felt so happy in this wonderful place and was already feeling so much better. Her parents could see that her health was improving rapidly. They could see her lungs taking deeper breaths of the clean fresh air more easily.

They agreed to stay. They found work easily – both working fewer hours for a lot less money but both feeling less stressed and having lots more time to spend with Penny. The house in the city sold very quickly and they bought the house next door to Nancy.

They now understood how important it was to live and work in a clean, unpolluted environment so they spent a lot of their time helping others to become aware of this. They became an inspiration to many other people who also began to understand that their values needed to change. Others also realised that fresh air, space and simple living led to a far greater quality of life. Money wasn't everything – that health and happiness were so much more important.

Earth changes

Earth became ravaged by humans. They didn't understand her. In their ignorance and lack of sensitivity they raped, burned, and pillaged their mother who gave so much nourishment.

Mother Earth was displeased. She had made an agreement before she was born whereby she committed to providing a sanctuary, a place of joy and pleasure, a place of beauty and abundance for all who came to live upon her. This agreement was in jeopardy through the ignorance of those humans who lived, generation after generation, upon her.

As the darkness descended into human hearts and minds as they lived their lives in fear and lack, the Earth also experienced that darkness. There is a corollary between the two.

Mother Earth realised that her agreement was in jeopardy – that she was not honouring the commitment she had made in another time and space. She began to feel guilt and shame for the path she had allowed to take place. She could see that something needed to be done so she gathered her forces and created her intent to change the pattern she had allowed develop.

When she felt the other planets in the solar system were in alignment with her purpose and intent she breathed in deeply and purposefully and with force and intent expelled her breath into the ethers. The energy force behind her intent was felt and picked up by other planetary beings. They had been preparing themselves for just this exact moment, as they knew conditions couldn't go on the way they were. They were willing to assist Mother Earth, Gaia, to regain her former status, that of being a playground for all galactic and human beings. They waited for the manifestation of her intent to materialise.

At the exact time the planetary energies were aligned in a certain way in relation to Earth, a massive earthquake occurred as Gaia signed deeply. She felt pain, anguish and deep sadness within her for what was about to occur, as she knew that much suffering would be experienced by humans. "However," she told herself, "it's important to look at the big picture – to be the beautiful home away from home that I committed to be. Perhaps humans will wake up after this tearing of my body and begin to understand and correct their ignorance."

Mother Earth's skin ripped asunder, her heart felt as if it would break as her body shook and heaved with inner disturbances. The ground opened, great chasms appeared, smoke bellowed out from her centre. Eruptions occurred simultaneously over many parts of her body. The rumblings went on for many weeks, gradually subsiding as her pain lessened.

All was now calm. Mother Earth rested. "Perhaps now people will stop their desecration of my body," she thought. "Perhaps they will appreciate their home and learn to treat it well."

Many did learn – many passed down to their children and grandchildren their understandings of what had taken place. They encouraged their offspring to value and respect the Earth and to treat her with love. They prospered and passed down to their offspring all that they had learned.

However, ignorance and darkness continued to be experienced by those who were totally focused on their material world. These people were greedy and they wanted power over others and over the land. They believed they had a right to do what they wanted on the land and that it was there to be used and abused however they saw fit. They taught their offspring not to value and respect the Earth. They taught them how to place purely material values above all else.

As generations passed a schism developed between the two belief systems. It was as if humans on Earth were divided into two distinct groups. Those who valued and cherished Earth and those who placed no value whatsoever on her freely given abundance and beauty.

Tension was again building up inside Mother Earth. She again felt the agreement she had made so long ago was not being honoured by her. She realised more action, perhaps even more disruptive than before, would need to occur in order for the darkness within and without to be released.

Again she re-committed to her life's purpose. She allowed her intention of rectifying the situation be sent out into the ethers. She watched the planetary alignments, preparing herself for what she knew was to occur.

When the moon was full great walls of water welled up inside her body. She cried great tears of frustration and sadness. Her tears became torrents. The fluids in her belly extended her so much they had to be expelled. Her frustration created underwater volcanoes to erupt under the seas and gush forth their lava and steam. This caused the waters to rise up and great tidal waves swept the shores of many continents.

Most places situated near the seashore were submerged by the great mass of water. The water travelled far inland, sweeping through towns and villages. All that man had built as memorials to his greed were washed away. Buildings crumbled, houses were swept away, vehicles were engorged and covered by the water in a matter of minutes.

The face of the land totally changed. Where there was dry land there was now lakes and rivers. The shoreline had moved inland by hundreds of kilometres. Many millions perished. Mother Earth had released her frustrations, her grief and sadness. She felt calm inside and rested peacefully.

"Would humans get the message this time?" she wondered. "Would they understand and learn from the experience? Would they begin to value and respect their home planet? Only time would tell."

Rachel and Mark

Rachel and Mark were beautiful young children. They were next-door neighbours and they loved playing with each other after school and on the weekends.

They were such good friends and enjoyed the same hobbies. As they grew older their parents could see how attached they were to each other and were a little concerned about the outcome of this attachment. As they developed into puberty they talked together about how their bodies were changing and what it felt like for both of them. They were quite open with each other and were totally unselfconscious and felt they had nothing to hide.

Their parents, however, began to imagine that the two friends would begin to investigate their sexual nature together, so each parent projected this thought onto the other parents. Their projected thoughts magnified until they imagined the young couple being actually engaged in sexual activity. They believed they had to stop this behaviour.

They became authoritarian and controlling. They told the young people they were not to see each other again. They gave no reason. Their fears and their own imaginings were drowning their love for their children.

Rachel and Mark were devastated and shocked by this unreasonable directive. They had never acted inappropriately. They had always been open and honest yet they were now prohibited from seeing each other. They both became sad, depressed and very unhappy. They each went to their room as soon as they came home from school and only spoke to their parents when spoken to. They didn't know what had happened to cause such an event to happen.

They lost interest in doing their schoolwork and their spark for living. They became ill because their spirits were down and so lost their natural immunity to fight disease. Their parents then became extremely worried. They loved their children and didn't want to see them ill and unhappy. They decided to have a discussion to try and work out the cause behind their children's illness and sadness.

Fortunately, their doctor was also their friend and had suggested to them some time go that it may have been their attitudes, beliefs and thoughts that were the cause of the children's depression and that perhaps they needed to look into themselves before they looked into external matters. The four parents talked about this and realised that it was their negativity, veiled behind their authoritarian behaviour that had actually caused the young people to become so depressed.

The parents could then see how, through lack of trust, they had caused such harm to befall their children. Because of their own fears and their inability to speak truthfully and openly to their children they had caused this tremendous rift.

They felt very sobered by this realisation, and then guilty. They realised they would need to right the wrong – to correct the injustice, not only for the children's sake, but for their own as well. They decided to get together that evening with their children and tell them the truth of their feelings. They knew this may feel embarrassing and awkward to them but they were willing to overcome this through their love for their children.

The meeting was arranged. The children were delighted to see each other again but distraught at the way the other looked. They were each a shadow of their former selves. They both looked weak, pale, gaunt and very thin. They hugged each other warmly – a light beginning to appear once more in their eyes.

Their parents then spoke lovingly to them, explaining how they had allowed their own negative projections and their lack of trust get the better of them. They said they felt their anxieties stemmed from the fact that they hadn't prepared the children for the onset of puberty by explaining the sexual urges and the responsibilities associated with it. They apologised to their children and said how saddened they were to see them become so weak and unhappy. They spoke lovingly and openly and Rachel and Mark felt their truth.

They then told their parents how betrayed they felt. How shocked and distraught they felt at the directive and how they couldn't understand the reasons. They told their parents how they had communicated openly and honestly to each other about their feelings and the body changes that were happening to them. They hadn't been secretive at all; each was simply interested in the other's feelings. There was no hidden agenda.

The parents then understood they had much to learn from their children. The children were demonstrating trust, openness and honesty. The parents felt humbled by the wisdom of their children and realised they had just learned a major life lesson.

Rachel and Mark once more played happily together after school and at weekends and both regained their good health very quickly. They were once again the bright, happy, loving and creative children they used to be.

Rundel

Once upon a time in a far distant land lived a young black- skinned boy whose name was Rundel.

Rundel loved to play outside in the trees. He built his own tree house and the ladder that took him up to the house. When he played in the tree house he imagined he was a king ruling all the land beneath him. He imagined he was an adventurer and his treasure was in a large box inside his tree house. He imagined he was Peter Pan, able to fly into different dimensions of time and space. Rundel loved being in his tree house, imagining all different scenes. He had lots of books up there as well and loved spending many happy hours reading his adventure stories.

One day, his father took Rundel to a different town. This was quite an adventure for him so he was eager to go. His father had business to attend to in the town and left his son in the park, asking him to stay there until he came for him.

Rundel looked around for some trees to climb and happily perched himself high into the branches of a large old tree. He had a book with him, so started to read.

He heard sudden noises underneath the tree and

saw two men fighting. One man had a package and the other man was trying to take it away. They were getting really angry, yelling and screaming at each other, and then one man hit the other.

The man that was hit took a knife out of his pocket and plunged it into the body of the man who had hit him causing him to fall down, bleeding profusely.

The man who had the knife panicked when he realised what he had done and ran off with the packet, but not before Rundel had had a really good look at him.

Rundel didn't know what to do because he wanted to obey his father and stay in the park but he also wanted to tell someone about what he had seen.

He saw a man and a lady coming towards the tree and so ran over to them and asked them to help him. They saw that he had dark skin and because they carried a lot of prejudice against people with dark skin they told him they didn't believe him and walked away.

Rundel felt very distressed by this, but knew that he needed to get help to the man under the tree and so didn't let his feelings of rejection worry him too much. He saw two younger men coming towards him, one white skinned and the other dark. He ran to them to ask for help. They asked Rundel to take them to the tree where the man was lying injured, which he did.

One of them knew a little about wounds and was able to bind up his bleeding body with a scarf. He asked the other man, the white skinned man, to go and telephone for help.

The two dark-skinned people remained under the tree with the injured man. A crowd began to form.

Some of the people were white skinned and they believed that these three people were all in a fight together simply because of their skin colour. Some of the crowd began muttering, "Dirty Nigger – Dirty Nigger," until these words echoed through to Rundel.

Because his actions were pure and good he couldn't understand why these people were getting more and more angry and totally ignoring the fact that there was an injured man lying on the ground. The crowd gathered some rocks and began throwing them at the three dark-skinned people and called them animal names.

Rundel became frightened and he wanted to run away. The young dark man who was with him had experienced this type of derision being heaped on him before for no reason, so he knew what to do.

He stood his ground. He stood straight and tall. He placed himself in front of the body of the injured man with the tree behind them both. He told Rundel to climb back into the tree and, as he was doing so and while the crowd was watching this, he firmly, confidently and lovingly told them what had happened.

He spoke simple words, just telling the story how it was with no embellishments. Because he spoke calmly and didn't go into blame, anger or defence, he was able to gain the attention of the crowd. They began to listen to him and soon they all felt his words in their heart. They soon forgot the fact that he had different skin and were able to simply see the true essence of the man.

They all felt humbled, sheepish, and one of them

offered an apology. The dark man thanked them for listening to him and asked them if they would help him. Most of the crowd had moved away by this time because they didn't want to stay there and face the man who had far more love and inner strength than they did. That was simply too much for them to cope with, so they moved away.

Three people remained to help, so one covered the injured man with a coat, another made a pillow for his head and held his hand. Another sang gentle, loving songs to him to keep his spirit bright.

Very soon an ambulance arrived with a doctor and the injured man was taken to hospital. A policeman spoke to Rundel and wrote down his story with the description of the man who had the knife and the description of the packet. He thanked Rundel for his observations and for his assistance.

Rundel felt he had made a friend with the dark-skinned man and asked him if he could see more of him. Rundel recognised the man's inner qualities and wanted to grow up with the same qualities inside of him. The man agreed to this and gave Rundel his contact address and phone number. Rundel's father returned whilst this interchange was taking place and the two men exchanged cordialities. A friendship was forming.

Rundel's adventures that day were even more exciting and unusual to anything he could ever have imagined. He certainly learned a lot about himself and about how other people think and react to situations. It was a very important life lesson for him.

the pixies

Once upon a time, in a land far away, lived a little pixie. She was so cute and cuddly and such a happy little soul. Her life was one of joy and wonderment. She loved playing in the sunshine with the flowers and plants. She loved the way the breeze blew the leaves and petals of the plants. She was such a happy and contented little pixie. She had many pixie playmates, all frolicking in the sunshine of the early morning.

One day, however, a big black cloud blotted out the sun. The pixies had not experienced this phenomena before, as all their days had been perfect. Something different and strange was happening to their world. The cloud became darker and darker and blotted out the light of the sun. The air became cold.

As you can imagine the pixies became frightened of this unusual happening. They all huddled together supporting each other to keep warm.

The black cloud seemed to hang quite close to their home – it seemed to be enveloping them. It felt like a huge, dark, damp hand was pressing down on them. They became more and more afraid and rushed around in a panic looking for somewhere to hide in order to escape this cold and dark.

They found an old tree trunk, which had rotted away on the inside, so they all huddled inside the tree trunk holding each other closely. They didn't like this blackness that had descended upon them. All the light had been blotted out. They couldn't even see each other.

After a while they calmed down. Some of them went to sleep hoping that when they awoke the dark cloud would have lifted. This was not the case however. This dark cloud was there to stay for sometime.

A few days passed by and the pixies realised the dark cloud was not going to go of its own accord. They began chattering amongst themselves to see if they could understand why this cloud had descended upon them. They realised that if they couldn't clear the black cloud and reach the light again then they would most likely perish, because without light nothing can grow and survive.

They began speaking amongst themselves putting forward their ideas as to why they had attracted this black cloud to their home. After a while they realised that most of the group had been behaving and thinking in a really negative way. Some of them had been feeling fearful because they had heard stories of black clouds descending on pixies from time to time and so they had begun to believe these stories.

Some of the pixies said that they were being very greedy, selfish and not wanting to share their games with others. Some other pixies said that they were jealous and envious of other pixies and felt black inside of themselves at times.

Eventually, the pixies realised that they all had been allowing black, dark negative thoughts and feelings to take over their being from time to time. They all admitted these dark thoughts and feelings to each other.

They could then see how these feelings had created a dark cloud to manifest in their external reality. They understood that the thoughts and feelings they had inside of them acted like a magnet to attract dark, cold things to happen outside of them.

There was a lot of chatter about this as some pixies still didn't want to admit they had these dark feelings and thoughts. One of the pixies said that she had looked outside and seen that the dark cloud had lifted a little, that there was more light and so they realised even more how true was their understanding.

The pixies that were still in denial of their dark thoughts and feelings then began to understand how this darkness inside of them attracted darkness outside of them. With the help of the other pixies they were then able to see how their black thoughts of envy, jealousy, hatred, fear and revenge created blackness inside of them and that, like a magnet, they attracted that to them in their external world. They then expressed their dark thoughts and feelings to the others, owning and being responsible for them – not in any way blaming anyone else for them. They felt so much lighter inside when they had done this.

All the pixies then joined hands in a circle and sang loving, happy songs together and felt a strong love flowing all around the circle. They hugged each other and spoke lovingly from their hearts. They then realised they could see each other more clearly and they rushed out into the garden to find that the big black cloud had lifted. The sun was now shining so brightly.

They vowed to always think light, loving thoughts from then on and if they ever felt dark feelings then to express them openly and honestly rather than suppressing them. They didn't want that dark cold cloud to descend on them ever again.

the Blue planet

Once upon a time, a very long time ago, planet Earth was created as a jewel in the galaxy. Her Creator called her the Blue Planet, as she seemed to shimmer in the solar system with such clear blue sparkling lights. She was pristine and clear in her youth. She radiated such beauty that many beings from all other galaxies were drawn to her for their holidays.

She was a haven of beauty. The beings that played upon her adored her and she in turn glowed even more brightly. She appreciated the love and care that was being shown to her.

Beings settled on planet Earth and civilisations grew and flourished. There was always so much food and water provided by Earth that the beings multiplied in numbers very quickly.

The beings cared for Earth, ensuring that they never abused her nor polluted her. They treated her with great respect and love and she in turn responded in kind.

One day, however, a fleet of foreign black flying ships appeared in the sky. These ships carried beings from a far distant planet who had heard about the wonders of planet Earth and who wanted to experience the phenomena for themselves. They landed their crafts in an uninhabited area and immediately started to rape and pillage Mother Earth.

They cut down precious trees that gave out so much oxygen. They burned great tracks of land, polluting the atmosphere and they dammed up watercourses to serve their own needs.

Mother Earth was shocked. She was still very young and had never experienced such abusive behaviour before. She couldn't understand why this darkness had come about.

The beings from the dark planet continued to plunder and they then moved into populated areas and continued the abuse. However, not only did they plunder and abuse Mother Earth but they raped, pillaged and abused the peaceful people who were living in communities.

The invaders had no thought for Mother Earth or for the other beings. Their only concern was to get – to take what they wanted for their own selfish ends. They wanted what the others had. They wanted the best lands, the best waterways, the best trees and they wanted more and more of it. They stopped at nothing to get what they wanted. They murdered, slaughtered, butchered and raped anything and everything in their way. They used their sophisticated weapons for control and domination of others.

Many beings now lived in fear of invasion. Many protective measures were built in an attempt to keep out the dark invaders.

Mother Earth was unhappy. Her rivers and streams

were very polluted. Her land was eroded and her atmosphere poisoned. She became very restless. She had all this scaring and illness inside of her. She felt ill. Never before had she experienced such pain.

Those people who lived upon her no longer treated her with respect. They no longer loved her and honoured her for the incredible nourishing and sustaining beauty that she was. She felt ignored, misunderstood, abused and sad. Her sadness then turned to anger. She began to boil up inside with unexpressed emotions. She wasn't willing to remain docile and subservient anymore. She was no longer willing to take the abuse.

Her belly boiled up with heat and she blew in rage. Volcanoes exploded all over the planet. Great seas of lava poured from her belly and ran down the hillsides, covering villages and towns.

Her rage was felt by all inhabitants on Earth. It was as if she had issued a warning, her message being: "I am willing to take so much, but I will not take any more of your continual abuse, your pollution, your total disregard for me. I want my lands to be clear and pristine again. I want my skies to be bright blue. I want my rivers and seas to be sparkling clean again and I will have my way."

Some of the inhabitants of Earth felt her pain and understood why she had demonstrated her anger and they told others of their understandings. However, the power hungry, greedy, dark inhabitants laughed at the idea and continued with their destructive ways. They continued to perpetrate fear, they continued to rape and pillage the land and communities. They continued to take, and take and take. They plundered the belly of Mother Earth, taking her precious metals and thus disturbing the natural energetic balance that had existed.

Internal disharmony was now being experienced by Mother Earth. Her energy meridians had been altered, she was weakening. She breathed in long and deeply and then expelled the feelings of sadness in a great gush of air and tears.

Great chasms opened up on her surface and the land shook with her sobs. Her tears flooded the rivers and seas and great tidal waves formed. The water engulfed the land.

Where there were settlements there was now ocean. Mountains arose from the seas to create new, clean, pristine land. The whole face of the planet changed. The clean waters lapped the new shores.

All the polluted lands were now under the sea. Once more Earth was the fresh, beautiful, blue jewel of the galaxy that she was created to be.

She rested, peacefully, recuperating from her long abusive ordeal. She knew she would be inhabited again. She knew she would most likely to abused again. However, she also knew she would act to protect herself more quickly the next time. She wasn't willing to allow such abuse to hurt her ever again.

Judy's Guardian Angel

It was a beautiful spring day when Judy decided to explore a different place in her garden. She lived with her brothers and sisters in a house in the country where she had lots of space to play her imaginative and inventive games. This day she elected to go to a place in the garden where she had never been before. The garden bordered on a rainforest and this part of the garden had often appeared dark and damp to her. It had frightened her in the past. Today, however, she felt brave enough to venture into this unknown territory.

She took her little dog with her for company and also some sweets in case she should feel hungry. As she was walking into the forest she noticed a great hole in the side of a mound and wondered what creature had made it. It seemed to be freshly dug, as there were scratch marks around it. Judy went further into the darkness, deciding to eat one of her sweets for comfort. She was a little scared but her curiosity was greater than her fear.

Suddenly, she tripped over a branch and fell to the ground, lying on the damp soil. Her heart was beating very fast, especially when she felt the presence of another around her. She stood up, turned around, but there wasn't anybody there. Her little dog was very quiet, yet very alert as if he sensed a 'something'.

Judith continued, moving deeper into the darkness of the forest. She heard birds singing sweetly to each other and saw butterflies flying around her. One landed on her shoulder. She was amazed at its beauty. She felt it was giving her a message – something to do with urging her on, helping her to overcome her fears of the unknown.

She saw a small clearing ahead where the rays of the sun were beaming onto a grassy patch. She decided to pause and sit a while under the tree, resting. The butterflies followed her and the birds moved to the tree above her. She felt they were her friends, guarding her on her path.

As she was resting her back against the tree she heard a voice that seemed to be coming from the tree itself. She turned to face the tree, placing her arms around it with her forehead to its trunk. The spirit of the tree spoke to her again, telling her that she had a special task to carry out during her lifetime. In order for the task to be accomplished successfully she needed to overcome her fears – to face them and move through them, rather than pretend they didn't exist.

The spirit of the tree sang her a little song, which brought tears to her eyes. The tears were of joy and gratitude. Her heart welled up with love at the words of the song. She was asked to remember this song and to sing it to herself daily as it was her own special prayer which would help her in times of need. Judith sang the sweet song to herself on her return journey, stopping to peer into the hole in the mound. She saw two bright eyes peering at he. However, she wasn't alarmed, as she knew she would be safe. She felt so protected by the birds and the butterflies and her heart was so light through singing her song.

Again she felt the presence of someone behind her. She could sense it. She could feel a different energy and she smelt a different smell. It smelt like fresh green apples. Again she turned around and this time she saw a faint outline of a beautiful lady with long blond hair smiling at her. Judy asked who she was and the lady seemed to reply in Judy's mind. She said she was a friend from a different dimension and that was why Judy couldn't see her clearly. She said she was always with Judy, watching over her and guiding her and that if Judith wanted she could think of her as her Guardian Angel. She went on to say that everybody has a Guardian Angel, or friends from different dimensions, guiding and assisting them. Some humans could see them clearly, some could hear them, and some could sense them or smell them. Often people would deny their presence because their minds were closed to knowledge of other dimensions. However, there are now more and more people who are willing to use their sixth sense to experience the mystical and unusual.

Judy wanted to hug her Guardian Angel but knew that wouldn't work. However, she thanked her and asked her how best to contact her when she needed to do so. The Guardian Angel told Judy to make sure her mind was clear and calm, to make sure the space around her was clean, to preferably go outside in nature and then ask for her presence with an open and loving heart. It was under these conditions that Judy would be able to see her. Should Judy's mind be troubled with dark thoughts and should her body be clogged with dark emotions then her perceptions would be dark and she would be unable to experience her Guardian Angel. The Angel would always be there but Judy would not be able to see her when in a negative state.

The Guardian Angel suggested that Judy make a practice of tuning into to her every morning upon waking, as it was then that her mind would be clearer and her energy of a higher vibration. She also suggested that Judy take a walk in the forest each day, getting to know all the forest creatures.

Judy's heart was singing. Her eyes glistened with joy and gratitude. What a wonderful gift she had received this day and all because she made the decision to burst through her fear of the unknown and face the darkness of the forest with courage.

Judy's experience stood her in good stead for the whole of her life. She travelled through her life with great trust, confidence and courage, knowing that she was totally protected by her Guardian Angel. She would always tell her friends and family that they too had Guardian Angels with them and they only needed to believe this was true.

Space Visitors

In a far away land, on a different planet, lived beings quite unlike us. They were a mixture of animal and human form. Some of them had heads like cows and bodies like humans, some of them had human-like heads and bodies like animals.

These beings were highly evolved in conscious understanding of themselves. They mostly lived in peace and harmony although occasionally disruptions would occur. Whenever sudden, unexpected events happened the beings knew that there was a challenge being presented to them by the Supreme Divine Creator to evolve to a further level of consciousness.

One day a spaceship landed near a heavily populated area. This was certainly an unusual event. This hadn't happened for many, many years, so the residents of this planet knew that big changes were to take place.

They were both excited and nervous. There were many strange looking entities in the spacecraft. They were more like humans. They had egg-shaped heads, very large eyes, hands and feet.

They alighted from the spaceship in pairs. They had

their hands in prayer position over their hearts, so the occupants of the planet knew the visitors had come in peace. There was much chattering amongst the residents. Lots of thoughts were whizzing through their minds.

The leader of the inhabitants moved forward to greet the unusual visitors. He too placed his hands in prayer position over his heart. He looked into the eyes of the being that was in front of him. He questioned him telepathically.

He asked what was their mission, what was their message? He said the visitors were very welcome on their planet and he trusted that they came in peace. He opened his arms wide to express to the visitors that they were indeed welcome and that the facilities of the city would be available to them.

The visitors then grouped together in a semi-circle and the local inhabitants then formed a semi-circle so that all were then joined into one large circle. This was a circle depicting unity.

The two leaders from the spaceship told their story. They said how they had been preparing for this excursion into space for some time. The idea had presented itself and they had been working at bringing it into manifestation. They had received the idea from the higher realms and they knew it was an impulse that needed to be acted upon. They said they didn't know what their task was after landing, except that they were to stay for some time and share their knowledge and their way of life.

The residents became really excited with this information as they could see that much evolution in consciousness would take place through the interaction with the space visitors.

This certainly was a great change. They knew they had a choice with this event. They could perceive it as an invasion and react in a defensive and self-protective, insecure way, or go with it even though it might bring up feelings of nervousness and agitation within them.

They were ready for change. They were willing to go with the excitement; they wanted to evolve. They didn't know what the outcome would be; they couldn't even imagine it. However, they knew that their positive actions today would be ensuring a wonderfully exciting future for them.

They opened their hearts and their homes to the visitors from outer space. They plied them with questions and they shared their customs with them. They learned a new and different way of living and relating. Some of it was so bizarre that they decided they were not able to go along with it at that time. However, for the main part the space visitors' ideas and way of living were an improvement to their own.

When the time came for the space visitors to leave there was much sadness for they had become a part of the residents' lives. Some of the space men had loving relationships with the local females and had implanted their seed. There would be babies born of the mixed races. These babies would be born with a higher consciousness to that of their mothers.

Evolution was occurring. The exciting and unusual circumstances were resulting in a societal swing, away from complacency and stagnation. A freeing up of old attitudes and patterns of behaviour was taking place. Vibrancy was developing. A more exciting way of living was manifesting, all because the residents chose to go with the new, with the unusual and to embrace it openly.

Their visions for the future were now wider and broader than ever before.

susan

It was a long time ago when Susan felt love in her heart. She had been very small, only about two years old, when she knew she was loved by her Mummy and Daddy, her Grandma and Grandpa. She could remember them all playing together in the garden on a beautiful sunny day. The birds were singing, a gentle breeze was blowing and there were lots of beautiful coloured flowers all around her.

Susan felt such love in her heart for the world of nature, for her family and for herself. That was the only time in her life she could remember feeling such joy and love.

The day after, her parents were killed in a car crash. Her Mummy and Daddy would never again be there for her. She felt as if her whole life was destroyed. She was bewildered and confused, hurt and sad. At such a young age she had so many emotions run through her. She felt abandoned by her parents. She was desolate and suffered a great loss.

She went to live with her Aunty who did her best to bring her up with love, however it wasn't the same. Susan's sadness increased over the years. Sometimes she was able to forget, to put her negative thoughts and emotions aside, but they would always rise to the surface again when she least expected them.

She married and had two children of her own and appeared to live a fulfilled life. She had material comforts. Her husband and children loved he. However, the dark place of emptiness was still inside her.

After the children had grown up and left home, she began to feel all the dark feelings again. She began to believe that her husband would abandon her as her parents had. She worried that he might have a car accident just like her parents. She began to have nightmares, becoming afraid to go to sleep at night.

All her childhood traumas were surfacing in her body and her mind. She went to doctors and all they did was to give her drugs to numb her mind.

One of her friends had had a similar childhood experience and had tackled her problem a different way. She had gone to natural healers, those people who knew how to work with the energy of blocked emotions and negative thoughtforms. Her friend had also started studying astrology and had found it to be an incredible helpful tool for healing as it showed quite clearly and precisely what the emotional or mental wounding was and how best to deal with it in order for life to be joyful and fulfilled.

Susan now had some options. She could choose to go the way of modern medicine, or she could choose to heal herself through gaining knowledge of how her own internal energies really worked by learning astrology and natural healing modalities.

As she had experienced modern medicine so far in

her life and had found it hadn't worked for her, she decided to become responsible for herself and her own emotional and mental states, so she became an avid student of astrology and metaphysics. The more she learned the better she understood herself and the happier she became. She could see that by delving deep into her soul self she could come up with many answers.

She began using natural healing methods. She practiced with crystals and found they were very healing to her. She used flower essences and she found these helped her move through difficult emotional times in her life with far greater ease than in the past.

She learned to discipline her mind through meditative practices and this training helped her change consciously her negative thoughts into positive ones. Her depression lifted. Her body responded and she became healthier.

She learned Reiki, a hands-on-healing system. As she learned all these different things she developed a far greater understanding of how the universal life force energy works. She understood that she had allowed her heart to be shut down and had placed barriers around it after her parents' death and these barriers were still in place. She committed to working with these energetic barriers consciously and to burst through her fears and the limitations she placed upon herself in her life.

She chose to change her negative beliefs consciously and formulated new ones that were much more uplifting and positive.

After some years of working on herself in this way

she decided to get a puppy as she felt her heart was still blocked and her love energy was still behind the closed doors of her heart. She and the puppy played a lot. He showed her unconditional love. She re-lived a childhood, only this time it was fun, playful and loving.

Her husband supported her in her efforts to bring healing to her heart. He could see the results of her internal work. Their relationship was becoming more loving and playful.

One day when Susan was sitting in her garden playing with her puppy she looked up and saw the beautiful blue sky, the trees whispering from the gentle breeze, the birds singing sweetly and the flowers brightly beaming all their different colours. She felt such a rush of joy and love to her heart. She felt engulfed with the feelings of love. Her heart opened – she felt it physically. She felt the barriers shatter. She felt at one with nature, with all of life. She was again the happy, joyful being that she once was, so long ago.

the king

Once upon a time, a long, long time ago, there lived a king in a great castle. The king was a very kind and benevolent man and ruled his land wisely and well. His family life was happy and he was a contented man. His spiritual life was also one of great joy to him as he meditated daily and allowed himself to be guided by his spirit guides from higher realms.

One day, a visitor from another country came to visit him. This stranger brought unhappy and disturbing news. He told of an army of men – many, many thousands – who were marching towards the kingdom with the view to taking control of the people and all the rich land.

The king was greatly disturbed by the stranger's news, thanked him for coming and bade him farewell. He decided to meditate on the problem and ask for guidance. He firstly wanted to know if the stranger's words were true. He had felt disturbed by them but in his heart he had felt confusion as to whether the stranger was really being truthful. He doubted the stranger's words.

Now the king had learned long ago to trust his intuition, that little voice that speaks so softly sometimes, and he had also learned that being in confusion and doubt always brings unsatisfactory results if action is taken when in this state. He also knew that if he chose to go into a state of fear, then that would only draw to him a dark and difficult situation. So he went into his meditation room in order to discern the real truth of the situation.

In his meditation he was given a vision, one which was symbolic but one which he could understand and interpret the symbolism.

The vision he was given was that of a lake, a calm and peaceful lake, where there were many trees bordering it and a beautiful green field beside the trees. It was a vision of tranquillity and peace.

The king knew that the water in the lake represented emotions, the trees represented strength and endurance and that the field symbolised peace and harmony. He knew then that he needed to be strong, to calm his emotions and choose to allow peace and harmony to continue in his life rather than choosing to feel fear. He felt well guided and content.

Some days later a group of men arrived at his palace. They carried guns and were very aggressive. They told him the same story that the stranger told and threatened him with their guns. He very calmly told them that he was not leaving but chose to stay and meet the army. The men threatened to harm his wife and family. The king held firm and stayed calm, just like the lake. He knew his wife and family were safe. He had sent them on a holiday well before the stranger had appeared. However, he didn't want the men to know this.

The men were becoming frustrated and angry because they couldn't make the king react to their aggression. They starting smashing some of the large pots that were in the entrance of the castle, venting their rage and frustration on destruction.

The king remained calm and steadfast.

Eventually the men tired and told the king the army would appear the next day and take over the kingdom and kill him.

Again the king went into his meditation room, sat quietly and calmly and asked for guidance. Another vision appeared, this time of a beautiful garden where there were many, many different flowers and plants. It was so beautiful. The king knew this garden symbolised the great beauty of planet Earth and the great gifts that God brought to the Earth so that people may stop, pause, see, and smell the perfection of the flowers. He then understood that he needed to pause, to stop, and to just allow Mother Earth to do her work naturally and all would be well.

The next day dawned brightly. The sun was shining and the air was crisp and clean. He could see a cloud of dust in the distance and watched it grow larger. He could soon make out many, many people coming his way. He sat calmly in the garden watching them approach.

Suddenly a dark cloud appeared in the sky. It was so heavy and dense it blotted out the light of the sun. Thunder rolled and lightning flashed, and then torrents of rain began to fall. The rain seemed to be heavier over the marching army. Lightning hit a tree in front of the marching men and it fell, blocking their way. The rain kept on pelting down. A river began forming, flowing down so swiftly, cutting through the road in front of the army.

The men were becoming frustrated, and that frustration turned into fear because they could see the king sitting in his garden peacefully, untouched by the deluge. They began to feel he might have magical powers.

The rain kept on coming. Lightning struck and another tree crashed down in the middle of the marching men. The river was flowing so swiftly by now that the invaders had difficulty in crossing it. Thunder rolled loudly with such force that the men became afraid. Some started turning back, deserting their leader. Others tried to run and hide behind the trees but the lightning struck again and again. The force of nature was unleashed. The rain was now so heavy that visibility was exceedingly limited. The men could only see a short distance in front of their feet. They were trapped.

The thunder cracked more loudly than ever. Eventually, the men turned back. They were not willing to stay and be subjected to the violence of the elements. They scrambled over each other, knocking each other down in their rush to escape. Their fear was so great. Some of the men who had fallen were trampled by hoards of others. Chaos reigned.

The king sat quietly in his garden watching and observing. He had totally trusted his vision. He totally trusted his intuition and his inner guidance and knew that all would be well for him so long as he allowed the forces from higher realms to aid and assist him.

He wondered with awe about the scene unfolding in front of his eyes. His faith in his higher guidance increased moment by moment.

He knew he would be tested again and that at a later date some other form of disturbance would come to him. He knew that he would also not react to the situation but allow his inner voice to speak to him. He knew without any doubt at all that he would always be guided in the best way provided he was in total trust and faith and allowed his inner guidance to work through him.

He watched the last of the men disappear from sight as the rain diminished in intensity. He observed that the thunder and lightning had stopped. He went into his castle and up to his meditation room in order to give thanks to God for assisting him.

the prince

Once upon a time, a very long time ago, there lived a prince in a far away land. This prince was so handsome and very, very loving. He excelled at sports and loved to compete in the village games. He always encouraged the others in the village to try harder and do better. He never ever abused his status in life.

He was getting to an age where it was time for him to find a partner in life as his father was becoming frail and weak and was not so able to run the kingdom anymore. The prince decided to go on a quest – a search for a companion. Someone who liked the same things that he did – someone who could help him run the kingdom when his father passed on.

He searched far and wide; travelling to many countries and meeting many people. However, he was not able to feel a special kind of love for anyone. He had been away from home for nearly two years by this time and so decided it was time to go back. He had become a little concerned about his father's health and felt very drawn to be with him.

His father was ill and was so delighted to see the prince although a little disappointed that he had not found a loving companion on his travels. In due time the father passed on and the prince became king of the land. It was a great responsibility, which he felt he really wanted to share with another. He decided to go away again, although not for so long this time, questing again to find a partner who could lovingly share with him the kingdom.

Again, he was unable to find just the right person. He had met many people but none had stirred his heart. He went back home deflated. He began to think there was something wrong with him. Why couldn't he feel for another what others seemed to feel?

He was attending to his daily duties and visiting many people in his kingdom and became aware that there was one person who was always there to support him. There was a young woman, very poor, who lived not far from his palace who always seemed to be tending to the many village problems. People used to go to her for advice, as she was a very loving soul.

The prince began to take quite a bit of notice of this young woman and of course she became aware of his attention. She became embarrassed and ill at ease but still she continued to do the village work.

One day he asked her to talk to him, to come to the palace so that they could communicate without interruptions from the villagers. She felt very, very apprehensive about this, thinking that he might be critical of her work in some way. She worried so much, beginning to feel more and more unworthy. As the day approached for her visit to the palace she began to be afraid – afraid that the prince might tell her to leave the village. She worried so.

At the meeting the prince realised she was nervous

and fearful and was able to calm her fears because of his loving nature. He asked her to talk about her work and her life and as she did so he felt himself being drawn to her. He could feel his heart being affected. He felt a warm loving glow inside of him.

He told her how he was feeling and asked her not to be fearful, just to relax and try and imagine he was an ordinary person and not a prince. She told him she had always felt a strong heartfelt pull towards him but had suppressed it because she was so poor and unworthy of love from someone such as he.

He realised that it had taken him all this time to understand that one doesn't need to travel to far distant places in a search for love. Love will be discovered when it is the right time, and that love has no boundaries. It is not determined by social or financial status – it simply is and all we need to do is allow it to unfold from within us.

He felt so blessed to have at last found his partner, his companion, someone who was there all the time. He had just been too blind to see.

timothy

Once upon a time in a far away land lived a small boy called Timothy. Timothy spent many happy hours each day playing with the animals of the forest. He loved to dance with the brolgas. He loved to sleep beside the forest creatures when they slept. The creatures all accepted him as part of their forest family.

Timothy grew up and as he became older he spent less and less time in the forest. He had many other interests now and spent a lot of his time reading and studying.

When Timothy was old enough he went to university and it was there that he met people with different ideas to him. Many of the people at university were interested in ecology and in preserving the natural environment but their only experiences were through book knowledge. They had no idea how animals really lived in the natural forests.

It soon became known that Timothy had spent much of his early childhood with the animals of the forest and so he was asked to be an adviser to many committees. Because of his knowledge obtained through his own personal experiences Timothy was able to assist the environmentalists to a great degree.

He became very influential in a world-wide environmental movement.

His childhood experiences shaped his life path.

new century

At the end of the nineteenth century many people were living a confused and unfulfilling life. They had little direction in their lives and little hope of abundance, happiness and joy.

They believed that the change of the century might bring about changes to their external life.

They planned great celebrations for the night when the change was to occur. Parties were organised and planned by millions of people all around the world. All were eager to welcome the new times, believing that suddenly, as if by magic, something in their lives would change for them.

The appointed hour came. There was much rejoicing and singing, and then – nothing. Not one thing had changed externally for them because they had not understood that for things to change they needed to change internally.

It was an anticlimax. People went back to their homes to address all the dark that was in their lives. Some of them 'woke up' to themselves and began changing their attitudes to life, consciously. Most of them kept on playing their same game – that of hopelessness, despair, confusion and unhappiness.

They did not want to look at themselves for cause of their lack. They continued to blame society, the government, the weather, their partner or their boss for the lack they experienced.

Another new century has begun. Will the same pattern repeat itself as has occurred many, many times before? Will people hope and expect that magical changes will come to them without any conscious effort on their part?

Time will tell.

Mabel

Mabel was feeling very tired and knew that she didn't have much more time on Earth. She sensed change coming. She sensed the stillness before the storm. She felt ready to go to her new home in a different dimension. Her body was worn and hurting in many places.

Her brother came to visit her, which brought her much joy. She had always felt happy with him. She respected and loved him and she knew he felt the same for her.

One day when she was hanging the washing on the clothes line she felt a terrible pain starting in her leg, moving up her body to her heart. It was like a vice crushing her heart. She tried to cry out but the pain was too intense. She collapsed on the ground.

Her brother sensed something strange happening and began to call out for her. When she didn't answer he became worried and went outside to look for her. He found her lying in a heap and could see that there was very little life left in her.

He called the ambulance and it arrived quite quickly.

Mabel was already in a different state. Her spirit

was leaving her body. It was going home to be once more with her soul family. Her spirit was freeing itself from all the dross and denseness it had collected during the incarnation and was already moving towards the light. Mabel's worn out body shuddered a little as she let go her last breath. She was at peace.

Her spirit was freed once again. Many lessons had been learned during the incarnation. It had not been an easy life. There had been relationship breakdowns and a great deal of poverty. However, Mabel had lived a very giving and generous life for others. She had always placed the welfare of others above her own and was always the first to lend a hand to someone in need.

She was not able to consider her own needs until the very last stages of her life and had felt frustrated and resentful because of this. However, that will be a lesson for another time and place.

Mabel's body will have rituals. Her family will grieve and some will feel remorse and even guilt but Mabel's spirit is free, healed and happy and at one with the Light. There is nothing for it to worry about, or to fear.

Mabel's evolutionary journey has now reached another stage of development. She is at peace.

penny

There was once a girl named Penny. Penny was a delightful child, full of fun and creativity. She was allowed a great deal of freedom in her childhood as her parents encouraged her spontaneous creative expression. They were always there for her emotionally so she grew up to being a very happy, loving and creative woman.

When Penny met the great love in her life and married him, she didn't realise that she had drawn to her a person with opposite characteristics to her.

Keith had been brought up in a very restricted and controlling atmosphere. There was duty and responsibility, but very little love. Keith was suppressed and didn't feel that sense of inner freedom that Penny had inside of her.

They were a good match as Penny was able to demonstrate to Keith how she played out her roles in a spontaneous, free, loving way and she could see how Keith played out the responsible and dutiful husband.

Of course, there was friction from time to time because Penny didn't want to learn to be responsible and consider others. She felt happy as she was and didn't see the need to change her attitudes. She thought responsibilities very boring.

Keith, on the other hand, found it difficult to let go of his controlling nature. He had learned at a very early age that it hadn't been beneficial for him to express his true essence of self, his loving, creative expression, and so he shut down and built up barriers around his heart. This is why he appeared aloof at times and cold and distant.

When Penny and Keith decided to have a baby they felt it important to talk about their different characteristics. Penny knew that having a baby would curtail her freedom, and so she began to fear. She also felt a weight, or burden, descending on her. It was a feeling she had never experienced and she didn't like it.

Keith was feeling excited about the new baby and he could feel strange sensations in his heart that he had never felt before. He could feel a softening.

The two of them talked about their new feelings quite openly. Keith assured Penny that he would be able to help her a lot in looking after the baby so that she didn't become resentful at the loss of her freedom. This meant such a lot to Penny and she began to drop her fears of the future. She assured Keith that she would love to have him nurture and care for the baby, as she knew this would help to open up his heart so much.

They planned the baby's arrival. Penny wanted Keith there so that they could both experience the joy of the birth together. They could unite and bond as a family.

Keith was afraid of being at the birth, partly because he subconsciously feared the opening of his heart. He knew he would experience powerful emotions that might overcome him and he wasn't sure he could cope with them. Penny knew that all the suppressed emotions he was carrying needed to be expressed, so she asked him to be there with her.

Iona was born on a beautiful clear morning when Penny and Keith co-operated to bring this beautiful loving soul into the world. Keith was overcome with emotion and cried from joy and the wonderful waves of love that engulfed him. He felt such gratitude for being present at such a miraculous event.

Penny also felt her joy and love and creative expression return to its highest capacity. The birth of Iona was the most wonderful, ecstatic, creative thing she had ever done in her life.

She felt blessed and content.

VIDEO

A long time ago Jim was born. Jim was a very quiet, lovable and gentle child. He rarely cried and just loved being on his back looking up at the clouds, watching their movement through the sky.

Jim grew older yet his love of cloud watching never left him. He always felt such peace when contemplating the heavens. One day Jim was asked to go to the movies with a friend. Jim enjoyed the movies and was looking forward to the experience. The movie was an animated children's story and Jim enjoyed it so much. He really got into the feel of the characters. He could sense himself in all of them.

Jim's friend had an idea about making a movie in video form and asked if Jim would be willing to help. Jim felt very drawn to this idea so they started to develop a theme. Jim liked to lie on his back watching the clouds and allowing imaginative thoughts to filter into his mind. He found that by relaxing totally new ideas would simply 'pop' into his mind.

Firstly, he realised, there needed to be a continuous thread – some story that linked the beginning to the end. There needed to be a flow. Secondly, there needed to be a plot, something intriguing that would be absorbing to the viewers. This plot needed to involve drama, laughter, fun, and fear. It needed to have a happy ending so that viewers would leave feeling uplifted and happy.

This seemed to be quite a tall order for Jim and his friend and they realised what a big undertaking it was to make a video. However, they still wanted to press on as the ideas kept on impulsing their minds.

They decided to base the story on that which they knew – perhaps the life experiences of one of them. This way they could create the story from their own life experiences rather than using another's experiences, or fantasies.

They had such fun writing the script and sketching the cartoon figures. Their journey of making the movie was a story in itself.

Once the format had been decided upon and the experiences formulated into words the movie flowed very easily. It was such an enlightening and fulfilling experience for them both. Because they put their heart and soul into making the movie it was a great success. The story inspired many people.

Many, many people were transformed through viewing the movie. Jim and his friend felt contented by the outcome.

Also by Barbara McDougall

Tara, Emissary of Light

A simple, easy to read and modern heart warming story of a light being from a far distant star system travelling to Earth, bringing gifts of peace to the local inhabitants. How she does this will hold your attention and keep you enthralled. "Written as an adventure tale along the lines of the *Celestine Prophesy*, this book will capture and hold your attention from cover to cover," Review – *Spiritual Links* magazine.

A Crack in the Cosmic Window

The uplifting, loving and practical spiritual messages in this book present new perspectives on life and open up new doorways of perception. A valuable bedside table book to use for daily inspiration and comfort. "These heartwarming messages bring solace to the soul and inspiration to the heart," Review – *Insight* Magazine

Gaia, Our Precious Planet

This soul stirring, heart opening, amazing story of human evolution will trigger many memories and touch a deep and long forgotten place within. It will challenge you to broaden your understanding of life on Earth. "I was enthralled and compelled to keep reading. I just could not put the book down. Truly a must read." – Melody, best selling author of *Love is in the Earth* series.

A Great Cosmic Joke

A light look at our evolution over time through the eyes of four different characters, all at different stages of awareness. This book is sprinkled with insights and revelations that will titillate the imagination of all readers. It is likely to stir each reader into seeing the Great Cosmic Joke of his or her own life! "Another wonderful book by Barbara McDougall, truly a being of light and love. *A Great Cosmic Joke is* truly another 'must read' – Melody, best selling author of *Love is in the Earth* series.

ALL BOOKS AVAILABLE FROM
SELF DISCOVERY SYSTEMS,

PO Box 249, Nerang, Queensland Australia 4211.

Fax: 61 7 5533 2297

at **$16.95** each.

Or at selected bookstores around the world.